Walter W Ward

Springfield in the Spanish American War

Walter W Ward

Springfield in the Spanish American War

ISBN/EAN: 9783337367404

Printed in Europe, USA, Canada, Australia, Japan

Cover: Foto ©ninafisch / pixelio.de

More available books at **www.hansebooks.com**

SPRINGFIELD

IN THE

SPANISH-AMERICAN WAR

BY

WALTER W. WARD

ILLUSTRATED

PRESS OF
ENTERPRISE PRINTING COMPANY
EASTHAMPTON, MASS.
1899.

To the
Officers and Men
of G, B and K Companies
Second Regiment Massachusetts
Infantry, U. S. V., and
H Company, Naval Brigade.

PREFACE.

In the Spanish-American war of 1898, Springfield rose to the occasion as she did in 1776 and 1861 and sent her youngest and best and bravest sons to the front. It was her sons who fought and fell at El Caney, the one battle of modern times where infantry, practically unsupported by artillery, captured a well fortified town and it was her sons who were in the lead in drawing the attacking lines so tightly about the city of Santiago that its surrender had to follow. It was her sons also who, on the high seas, on a fast auxiliary cruiser, did faithful service as a portion of the navy and had the satisfaction of doing their share in remembering the Maine by sinking a Spanish transport and a gun boat. Her sons fell on the battlefield and died in the camps and hospitals after enduring as soldiers, the hardships and toils of one of the shortest yet most important and bloodiest campaigns in history and of the honors of that war, Springfield claims a goodly share for herself.

In the near future a monument, the funds for which have been contributed from near and far, will be erected in Springfield to the memory of the officers and men of the Second Regiment, Massachusetts Infantry, U. S. Volunteers who fell or died in the Spanish war. On that monument, whatever form it may take, will be inscribed the names of Bowen, Harry and Paul Vesper, Bearse, Noone, Piper, Boone, Jones, Richmond, Packard, Kelly, Moody, Burnham, Malone, Burke, Little, Stetson, Creley, Lyons and Morehouse. But their names have long before this been permanently inscribed on the hearts of their comrades and in no place are they more secure. They died for the flag, the highest honor possible to an American citizen. This volume is written in the attempt to portray as clearly as memory serves what these men and their comrades did in the war with Spain. While not actually a history, the intention has been to show as clearly as possible the people of Springfield what it was their sons and brothers and friends in her four organizations at the front went through in their short campaign.

Springfield, Nov. 1899.   W. W. W.

LIST OF CONTENTS.

CHAPTER.		PAGE
I.	Which is preliminary to those which follow it,	9
II.	Which tells about the calling out of H company, Naval Brigade,	14
III.	How G, B and K companies went to South Framingham,	19
IV.	Wherein is told how we were transformed from "tin" soldiers into the real article,	25
V.	We get orders to leave for the sunny South and obey them,	32
VI.	We go to the Southland and begin to find out where we are at,	38
VII.	We stay in Ybor City and then enjoy(?) life on the transports in the harbor,	44
VIII.	We have a lovely sail on the palatial Knickerbocker and reach Cuba without mishap,	51
IX.	Wherein is related our landing at Daiquiri and some things which subsequently happened,	59
X.	In which is to be found the tale of Crab Hollow and some other things,	68

XI.	Which tells how we got ready to take the town of El Caney,	76
XII.	Wherein is related some events which happened to us on July first,	84
XIII.	We learn some more things about the art of war as conducted in these days	94
XIV.	We continue our education in the art of war and learn a few things,	106
XV.	We have to face another enemy more deadly than the Spaniards,	119
XVI.	Our voyage homeward on the death ship Mobile,	129
XVII.	We and our friends enjoy ourselves at Camp Wickoff, Montauk Point,	136
XVIII.	In which is told how we prepare to quit Uncle Sam's service,	143
XIX.	We become plain citizens once more and square accounts with Uncle Sam,	151
XX.	Wherein is narrated the adventures on the high seas of Springfield's sailors,	161

Roster, - - - - - - - 172
The Roll of Honor, - - - - - - 178
Springfield's Dead Heroes, - - - - - 180

THE CAMPAIGN IN CUBA.

Experiences of Co's G, B and K, M. V. M., and H Co., Naval Brigade in the war of 1898 and record of its service in the operations against Santiago.

BY WALTER W. WARD.

CHAPTER I.

WHICH IS PRELIMINARY TO THOSE WHICH FOLLOW IT.

WITHIN the few years preceding the fateful one of 1898 a decided impetus had been given the military spirit in Springfield by the stationing of two additional companies of the state militia in this city. To the already organized companies, G and B of the Massachusetts Volunteer Militia, had been added K company, the company of that name in Amherst having been disbanded and its letter transferred to Springfield. The organization in this city of a company of the state naval brigade and the building of a handsome and commodious state armory helped to place the militia of Springfield on a higher level in the public interest and regard than had previously been the case.

Springfield has always been rich in military tradition. Her earliest sons helped fight the Indians who disputed the right of the first settlers to the lands they roamed over in the fertile Connecticut valley; they had served in the Colonial wars and Springfield blood was shed in the Revolutionary war. Soon after this war Springfield was the scene of one of the episodes of Shay's rebellion. In the Civil war she sent her full quota and more of her young men to serve under the flag and after the war the ranks of her militia companies were always kept filled with her best young men. Undoubtedly the presence here of a United States military post and the famous Springfield arsenal has done much to aid in keeping up the military spirit.

For long years, reaching back to a time before the rebel guns opened fire on Fort Sumter, Springfield's one military company was the City guard, which after being attached to several of the state militia organizations became under the final reorganization of the state troops B company of the Second regiment of infantry, M. V. M. In 1868 a number of the veterans of the Civil war organized the Peabody guard which was attached to the Second regiment as G company. Both these companies were always composed of good material and maintained a high place in the state militia, not only for excellence in drill but in discipline and marksmanship. The location of regimental headquarters here several years ago aided in making military interest more rife than for some years.

With four companies of militia instead of two, with headquarters and a fine new armory in place of the more or less unsatisfactory quarters previously occupied and with public feeling more united in their support than it had been for years the militia of Springfield felt they had entered upon a new period and it was one, which though they did not then realize it, was to soon test the courage and soldierly qualities of many of the officers and men of the Springfield militia.

But with this then unknown the spirit of soldierly pride and loyalty to their organizations led officers and men to constant striving to be at the top or as near the top as possible, of the militia of the state in all things soldierly. In drill, in discipline, in knowledge of guard duty, in marksmanship and in all the other details that go to make up a good soldier there was assiduous practice and to the furtherance of that end many of the ceremonial features of military life, to which great importance had previously been attached, were discarded as far as possible. This was thoroughly in line with the policy of the state military authorities and its value was to be proven sooner than was anticipated.

It did not take a very far seeing mind to realize in the fall of 1897 and the first two months of 1898 that matters with regard to the policy of the United States in the affairs of Cuba might soon produce a crisis so acute that the military power of the Republic would have to be called upon. Certainly it was realized by the militiamen and the progress of events from the beginning of 1898 to the night of the destruction of the Maine was by none more closely watched than by the men who gathered in the company rooms in the armory each night.

When it was known definitely that the long anticipated call to arms could not be much longer delayed the local militia was never in finer fettle. The ranks of every company were filled and soldierly enthusiasm ran high. New arms, not comparable of course with those of the regular army but better than any previous militia armament, had been issued and the equipments and uniforms were in good and serviceable condition. Applications for enlistment were so numerous that had there been eight companies instead of four their ranks could have easily been filled up.

It was on the 29th of April, 1898, that the call for troops came to Springfield. On the 23d President McKinley had issued the first call for troops and six days later Gov. Wolcott designated Col. E. P. Clark of the Second as one of the six commanding officers to raise a regiment of volunteers for the United States service. It was provided that members of the militia were to be given the preference in enlistments to the volunteer regiments, the residue being made up by enlistment of other citizens. The Second was ordered to report at the state camp ground at South Framingham on May 3 for muster into the United States service. April 29th fell on Friday and May 3 on Tuesday of the following week so that there was not any too much time in which to enlist men for the companies and get everything in readiness for service. But what time there was on hand was so well utilized that promptly at the hour ordered on the morning of May 3d the three Springfield companies were at the armory with full ranks and fully equipped, all the state property and equipage not needed packed up and ready for shipment to the state arsenal.

Every officer of the three companies and fully 70 per cent. of the men who had been in their ranks in the militia service was on hand. Capt. John J. Leonard of G, a veteran in the militia, was at the head of his company and with him his two lieutenants, T. A. Sweney and E. J. Leyden. Capt. Henry McDonald of B company, a veteran both of the regular army and the militia, and his lieutenants, William L. Young and Harry J. Vesper were on hand promptly and so was Capt. W. S. Warriner and Lieutenants P. C. Powers and Harry H. Parkhurst of K company. All three companies were proud of their officers and they had every reason to be.

And here a little digression. No effort of any kind was made to transfer as absolute unities the companies of militia into companies of United States Volunteers. It can truthfully be said that no man was asked to go to South Framingham by the officers. On the contrary Col. Clark and the company officers were all careful to impress upon the men of the militia that their volunteering into the service of the United States was purely a voluntary and personal matter with them. There were dozens of instances in which the officers realized that the sacrifice was such as some of their men should not make. There were men with families dependent upon them or so otherwise circumstanced that it was best for them not to go and these men were talked to candidly and kindly and dissuaded from putting their names on the enlistment rolls. It was a volunteer movement purely and simply and the Second was in the highest sense of the word a volunteer regiment.

Long before the orders for mobilization at South Framingham were issued preparations had been made to the end that Massachusetts might be ready to respond to the first call for troops from the national government. Early in April Gov. Wolcott had constituted some of the officers of the state militia as his advisory board in matters relating to the part Massachusetts would take in the war. On April 20, Col. Clark of the Second and some of his field and staff officers were called to Boston in consultation with the governor and on the 24th Gov. Wolcott in his capacity of commander-in-chief of the military and naval forces of the state issued an order calling upon the militia to hold themselves in readiness for duty within 24 hours.

CHAPTER II.

WHICH TELLS ABOUT THE CALLING OUT OF H COMPANY, NAVAL BRIGADE.

MEANWHILE, and while the infantry were getting in readiness, Springfield had already sent some of her sons on duty. The naval arm of the service was in a far more advanced state of preparation than was the army and it was the general opinion that of necessity the war would be one in which the navy would take the most prominent part, leaving but little for the land forces to do except garrison duty. Springfield had taken great pride in her company of the Massachusetts naval brigade since its organization and expected great things of it in the event of its being called upon for duty.

On April 2 came the first intimation that Springfield was to be called upon for men. Although war had not been declared and strenuous efforts were being made to head it off by the peace-at-any-price men, the navy department had set about getting into commission all the vessels that it could. At the League Island navy yard, Philadelphia, there lay a number of the old time monitors, some of them having been moored there since shortly after the close of the civil war, and it was decided to put them into condition for harbor defense purposes. Two were to be assigned to Boston harbor and on April 2 came orders to Lieut. J. K. Dexter, the commander of H company naval brigade, to proceed to the

League Island yard as an officer of one of the monitors. Lieut. Dexter left that night and remained on duty at the yard until April 16, when he returned to bring down the detail of his company which was to form part of the crew of the single turreted monitor Lehigh. It was not until April 17th that the Lehigh detail left for the Philadelphia navy yard although there had been many rumors as to when the men would go and the quarters of the company at the state armory were filled every night with the men and their friends. On the 16th Lieut. Dexter returned unexpectedly from Philadelphia and at once set about getting his detail together. It was on Sunday, but with the aid of the alarm list system, the telephone and special messengers the men were soon notified and assembled at the armory. The detail as finally made up was: Lieut. Jenness K. Dexter; Chief Boatswain's Mate, Frank H. Bowen; Boatswain's Mates, Robert T. Whitehouse, A. T. Wright; Gunner's Mate, F. W. Baum; Coxswain, W. S. Johnson; Acting Coxswain, S. L. Ruden; Quartermaster, W. A. Sabin; and Seamen Paul H. Lathrop, R. H. B. Warburton, W. F. Bright, R. P. King, A. Mellor, A. N. Luce, and L. E. Ladd. The detail marched to the union station at about 8.30 and took the 9 o'clock train for New York, receiving an ovation as it passed through Main street and again at the station as the train pulled out.

On the same day Lieut. (junior grade) Henry S. Crossman, who was in command of the company during the absence of Lieut. Dexter, received orders from Capt. Weeks of the naval brigade to hold himself in readiness to proceed to the Brooklyn navy yard and there report to Admiral Bunce, commanding the yard, as watch officer of the auxiliary cruiser Prairie to which the Massachusetts naval brigade was to be assigned. Lieut. (junior grade) W. O. Cohn was ordered to be in readiness to proceed to Boston and report for duty on the U. S. S. Minnesota, Ensign W. S. Barr was ordered to be in readiness to go to the Brooklyn navy yard as one of the watch officers of the Prairie and Ensign Fred T. Ley was ordered to the same ship as watch officer and Captain's clerk.

On April 22d these orders were changed, Lieut. Cohn and Ensign Barr being ordered to report for duty on board the monitor Lehigh on her arrival in Boston harbor.

On April 23d, Lieut. Crossman received orders to proceed with the remaining men of H company to the Brooklyn navy yard there to go on board the Prairie as part of her crew during the war. These orders were received on the morning of the 23d and as soon as it became known about the city that the men were to go, the war time scenes of 1861 were re-enacted. It was at first planned to have the company take an early evening train but as Lieut. Crossman found they could go just as well on the early morning train from Boston he decided to take that, thus giving the men more time in which to settle up their affairs and get everything in readiness for leaving.

Information about the Prairie had already been pretty well disseminated about the city. It was known that she was formerly the fast steamer, El Sud, of the Morgan line and was capable of doing excellent duty as one of Uncle Sam's auxiliary cruisers. At the time she was in the Brooklyn navy yard being changed over from a passenger and freight vessel to a war ship and the job was requiring longer time than had been anticipated.

The quarters of H company and the state armory were the busiest places in Springfield that afternoon and evening. The "jackies" were getting their dunnage rolls and equipment together and relatives and friends were on hand to say farewell and see their "boys" off. Owing to the time at which the company had orders to leave the armory, 1.30 a. m., it was hardly expected there would be much of a crowd on hand to give the command a suitable farewell but this was a mistake. Long before the hour at which the company

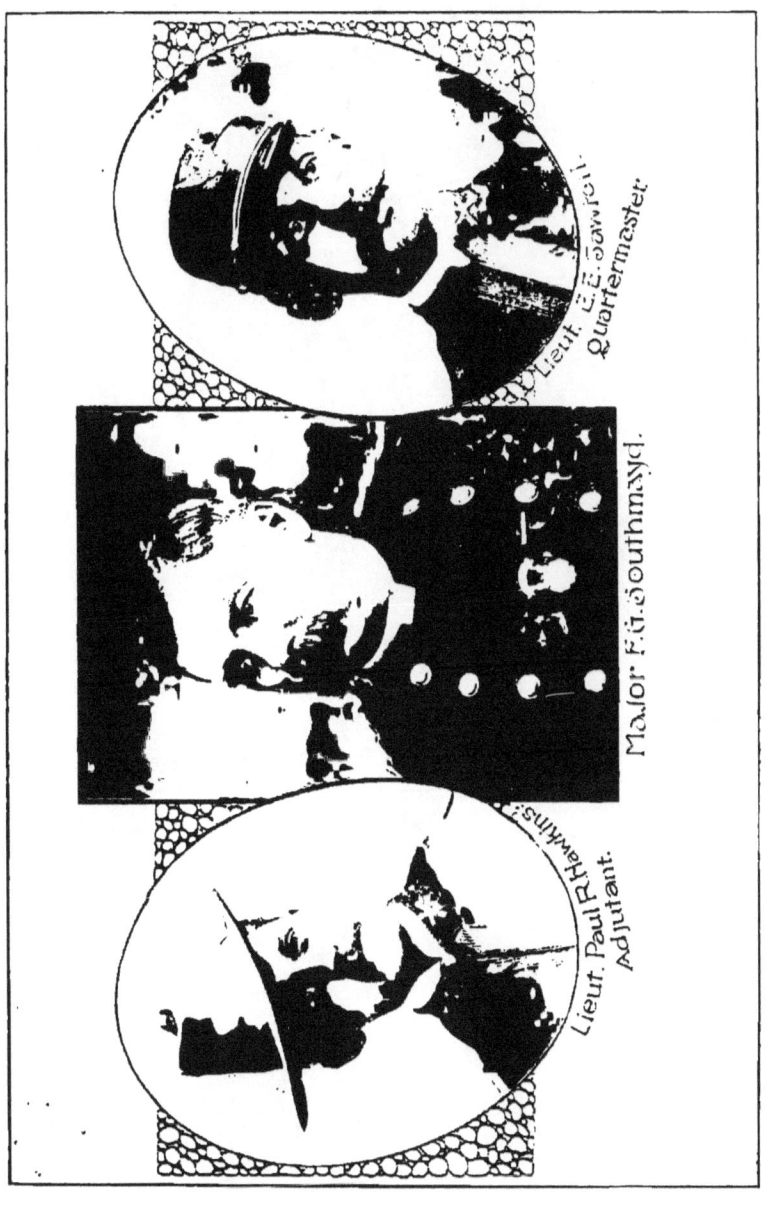

was to leave the streets leading to the union station were crowded and more enthusiasm was shown than had been the case in Springfield for many a day. It was at 1.30 o'clock in the morning of the 24th that the company, fully armed, equipped, in the regulation uniform of the jackies of the navy left the armory and marched through Main street to the union station to take the 2.20 train for New York, special cars for the company having been attached to the train. In spite of the lateness of the hour Springfield's citizens and the relatives, friends of the company were determined not to let the command leave the city without some demonstration. All night long up to the time for leaving the armory the building was filled with the relatives, friends of the members as well as those who while not bound to them by any intimate ties yet wished by their presence to show appreciation of the spirit which had prompted the young men to answer their country's call, even though it involved sacrifices hard indeed to make.

From midnight until the hour for departure Main street was well filled with a waiting crowd and when the company marched from its armory, swinging into Main street, a cheer went up which was continuous until the train had borne the company out of sight of the assembled thousands. Rockets and colored fire lent brilliancy to the march and as the station was neared the denser grew the crowd until it was with difficulty a way was cleared for the company. Thousands, men and women, had gathered at the station and it was a scene worthy the pencil of a great artist, that farewell as the men marched up and boarded the cars with military precision. There were cheers and good wishes, personal farewells and tears, all commingling in one mass of sound that the station space had never heard before. But as the engine bell rang and the train began to move with slowly increasing swiftness out of the station all sounds merged into mighty cheers, which rose thunderously from the thousands of people. In that uproar of cheers were submerged for the time the sobs of a few whose near and dear ones were on the train.

So Springfield sent her first contingent to serve under the old flag in the war against Spain.

CHAPTER III.

HOW G, B AND K COMPANIES WENT TO SOUTH FRAMINGHAM.

WHILE the naval militiamen of Springfield were being sent off to their places of duty amid the cheers of the people plans for the mobilization of the land forces of the state were going on apace. The call of President McKinley for troops was issued on April 23 and six days later on April 29, Col. Embury P. Clark of the Second Regiment of Infantry, M. V. M., was designated by Gov. Wolcott to raise a regiment of volunteers to answer the President's call as one of the four volunteer infantry regiments assigned to Massachusetts. On the same day Col. Clark was ordered to have his regiment report for duty at the state camp ground, South Framingham, at noon of May 3d, he being also ordered to assume command of the camp formed there by the four volunteer regiments.

On receipt of these orders Col. Clark immediately notified his field and staff and company officers and from that time on everything at the state armory was done with a snap and a jump. Only a few days remained before May 3d, for that day fell on Tuesday, and it was Friday afternoon when the orders were received. Under the call the company strength for infantry was fixed at three officers and 74 enlisted men, but had it been 174 instead of 74 there would have been but little trouble in filling up the ranks. More men were anxious to enlist than there were places for and a hard problem for the company officers to face was that of discouraging and rejecting applicants for enlistment most of whom pleaded for the privilege as strongly as a ward politician does for a paying office. On an average about 75 per cent. of the men in the militia companies enlisted in the volunteers and it is only just to state that a good number of those who did not were "talked" out of it by their officers who realized, perhaps better than the men themselves, that going to the front meant more sacrifices than men with dependent families or relatives should be called upon to make.

Meantime all was hurry and bustle at the state armory but order soon came out of all the apparent chaos and early on the morning of Tuesday, May 3d the local field and staff officers of the regiment and G, B and K companies, thus formed in the order of seniority of their captains, stood in the big drill shed, in full marching uniform with knapsacks packed and overcoats rolled up on them looking soldierly, and ready for whatever duty might call them to do.

It was a dismal morning in more than one way. A drizzling rain fell at intervals and there was gloom in many hearts among the crowds of people lining Main street and the union station and its approaches. Though not a shot had yet been fired in actual conflict between the United States and Spain on land and Dewey's great victory at Manilla had been won without the loss of a single American life, yet the people were beginning to understand that the grim realities of war might be brought home to them and this thought had its influence in repressing any too enthusiastic demonstration.

But there was a demonstration, nevertheless. Outside the armory were hundreds of spectators, including relatives and friends of the boys and awaiting them were the members of E. K. Wilcox post, G. A. R., the veteran corps of G company and some veterans of B company, all headed by the Second Regiment band to act as escort for the companies as far as the union station.

Shortly after 8 o'clock the troops left the armory and headed by the escort marched through Main street and around Court square to city hall, where the column was reviewed by Mayor H. S. Dickinson and the city government. Thousands of people were massed here and there was some cheering. The fire department boys at headquarters on Pynchon street saluted the troops with a small cannon and on the rest of the way up Main street to the station there was some cheering but not any too much.

At the corner of Main and Lyman streets the escort halted and formed in line. As the companies marched by the old soldiers of the civil war gave us three cheers, in which the militia veterans joined. The remainder of the march to the station was through a close packed crowd of men, women and children. There was some cheering, but as the soldier boys began to file into the waiting cars of the special train sobs and tears broke out from many of the women and as the train pulled out a few moments after 9 o'clock tears were more in evidence than cheers. As one of the boys put it, "They sent the naval boys off with cheers and kept the tears for us."

This feeling was augmented by the enthusiasm with which the people of Worcester sent their three companies off. When our train pulled into the Worcester depot we found the building jammed with people, some perched upon the tops of standing engines and cars and the Worcester companies were so surrounded with people it was at first hard to tell where they were. When our special stopped and the Worcester men began to board it a volume of cheers went up that was almost enough to take the roof off the building. Everyone was cheering apparently and those who were not were so few in number that it was impossible to distinguish them.

After leaving Springfield there were small crowds at every station between there and Worcester and though the train did not stop there was much cheering and waving of hats. This was repeated during the run from Worcester to South Framingham.

It was shortly before noon when we reached South Framingham and marched to the camp ground amid the cheers of the townspeople. Reaching there the companies were dismissed to quarters and dinner, which the company caterers had ready for us, we not going on government rations until some days later. A majority of the boys had been in camp at South Framingham before but this was different. A state militia encampment is one thing and a camp of United States volunteers is another. The old familiar wall tents were there but without the customary big blue chests in which were always stored much that was good in the way of refreshment for tired and thirsty militiamen. There was a trifle of added sharpness to the commands of officers and non-commissioned officers and there were various other little things which combined to show us that we were on the way to be the "real things" instead of "tin soldiers" as we had been dubbed in our militia days.

"Physical examination of recruits" was the rock on which the desires of many of us to get at the hated Spaniards were to split and the rock began to show itself that very afternoon when A of Worcester was ordered over to brigade headquarters for examination. Before the shades of evening fell thirteen of its men had been rejected by the examining surgeons and as bad news always spreads through a camp with greater rapidity than good, many of us were wondering whether we would meet the same fate or not within the next few days.

All the line officers and 75 per cent. of our men in the militia had come with us while there were more than enough "rookies" to fill out the quota. The recruits were, some of them, in uniform and a number had formerly been in the militia service, so that they took kindly enough to the opening of camp life. But as the militia companies had only been composed of 58 enlisted men there were not uniforms enough at the time to equip the extra men and some of the "rookies" looked odd and felt it in their civilian attire. More than one practical joke was played upon them before "taps" sounded, but the great majority of the men were tired enough to get to quarters and hug their luxurious mattresses before the bugles sounded the last call of the day.

Of the field and staff and non-commissioned staff resident in Springfield and vicinity not all came to camp. Col. Clark and Major Southmayd were on hand as was Lt. Paul R. Hawkins, the regimental adjutant. Quartermaster Colson of Holyoke did not come and to his place was appointed Corporal E. E. Sawtell of K company. Major Brown of Adams, the regimental surgeon and Lt. J. T. Hendrick of Springfield, assistant surgeon did not volunteer and a new surgical staff was appointed, consisting of Dr. Henry T. Bowen of Springfield as major and surgeon, Dr. Ernest A. Gates of Springfield and Dr. John S. Hitchcock of Amherst as assistant surgeons with the rank of first lieutenants. Dr. Hitchcock was a member of I company when appointed.

There were several changes in the non-commissioned staff. Corporal Robert N. Ingersoll was made sergeant-major vice Paul Norton and Ross L. Lusk quartermaster-sergeant vice Melville Snow of Holyoke. Three hospital stewards instead of one were assigned to the regiment, and the appointees were Ulysses G. Fortier of Holyoke, S. H. Greenberg of Boston and Edson P. Howes of Springfield. No color sergeants were provided for in the volunteer regiments and these positions were filled by detail.

It was a matter of much regret that no place was provided for the paymaster and inspector of rifle practice. In the Second as a militia regiment these positions had been filled respectively by Lieut. A. C. Edson of Holyoke and A. E. Taylor of Chicopee Falls but no such positions were provided for in the volunteer service and these officers were forced to remain behind.

The first guard mount of the camp was held in the afternoon with First Lieut. P. C. Powers of K company as officer of the guard. So closed our first day at South Framingham.

CHAPTER IV.

WHEREIN IS TOLD HOW WE WERE TRANSFORMED FROM "TIN" SOLDIERS INTO THE REAL ARTICLE.

IT did not require many days of camp life at South Framingham to convince about all of us that we were there strictly for business. The weather was rather cold and there were a few flurries of snow although it was in May. The nights were so cool that huge fires of wood were built on the color line each night and around these the men gathered spending the time in singing, story telling and in wondering how soon we would start for the front and just what part we of the Second would take in subduing the pride of the haughty Spaniard.

But little in the way of drilling was done at first, but after a day or two the work of whipping the "rookies" into shape was begun, the process being the simple one of having them fall in with the company and learning the drill as best they could. Squad drills were also carried on and it was during these that the raw material was best worked up.

Hardly had the regiment arrived in camp before regulation United States army blankets were issued to the men and issues of rubber blankets, "working suits" of brown canvas followed.

Private Pomeroy of K company was the first of the Springfield men to be taken ill. He had not been feeling well before leaving home but pluckily made up his mind to go with

c

his company just the same, and would not admit his illness. Soon after arriving in camp his condition became so serious that the surgeon was called to him and Pomeroy was found to be suffering with tonsilitis. He was removed from the camp to a hospital in South Framingham, but while there scarlet fever developed and he was sent home as soon as he had recovered sufficiently to be able to travel. Pomeroy felt much worse over his inability to go with his regiment than he did over his illness, serious as it was.

The physical examinations soon made many sore hearts among the boys in camp, although the results of some of them were extremely satisfactory to the parents, relatives or friends of some of the would be soldiers. They were in charge of Capt. Bushnell U. S. A., who was assisted by the surgeons of the volunteer regiments in camp. B company was examined on Wednesday, the day after our arrival in camp and before sundown fully twenty men, including some of the oldest and best men of the company had been rejected for one cause or another. The commissioned officers of the regiment were also up for examination the same day, and among those rejected was First Lieut. Thomas A. Sweeney of G company and one of the most efficient and popular officers of the regiment. His rejection was a hard blow to him for he had set his heart on going with his men and to be rejected for what he considered to be a trivial cause was worse to him than being hit by a Spanish bullet. His grief was shared by his fellow officers and men, by whom he was exceedingly well liked. His place was filled by William C. Hayes, a former first lieutenant of the company.

Lieut. W. L. Young of B company was officer of the guard on Wednesday, and among the incidents of his tour of duty that night was the rather unusual but efficient method by which a private of G company who had been placed on a somewhat remote post relieved himself from further duty after walking his post only a short time. The aforesaid private concluded that he would be much more comfortable in his tent with his "bunkies" than walking his post for the remainder of his two hours, and so proceeded to the guard house, placed his rifle in a corner and announced to the officer of the guard "I'm relieved." Before Lieutenant Young could recover from his astonishment at the new method of getting out of guard duty, the private had gone to his own quarters where he slept peacefully for the remainder of the night.

The results of the physical examinations were to "throw out" many of the best men in the three Springfield companies, and as this was not at all satisfactory to their captains, some vigorous "kicking" resulted. In many cases men were rejected for trivial causes, but as the result of vigorous objections to the policy, made by Captains Leonard, McDonald and Warriner, a number of the rejected men were re-examined and the majority of them accepted. In some instances more than two examinations were given the same man, and an instance where grit and a determination to go with his company got the best of the examining surgeons was the case of Sergeant Richard H. Bearse, better known as "Dickie." He was twice examined and rejected but through his efforts, aided by those of Capt. McDonald, he was given a third trial and passed.

Could those people who had been for some years in the habit of sneering at the militiamen as "tin soldiers" have seen the way in which the rejected ones took their fate they would have changed their minds as to the soldierly calibre of the men of the Second. It was easy to tell the rejected ones as they came across the parade ground from the surgeon's quarters, many of them with tears in their eyes, all with downcast faces, because their bodies had not been strong enough to let them go with the regiment. Their hearts were strong enough to go to the front and fight for the flag but the government demanded stout bodies as well as stout hearts, and so, many were refused. It was not always in tears and "blue" looks that the rejected appeared from the examining rooms. Often a rejected one would emerge, uttering sarcastic and profane remarks as to the amount of surgical knowledge possessed by the examiners, and their qualifications generally, and some of the men exhibited a versatility of language in discussing their rejection and the surgeon who was responsible for it only possessed by men of genius.

The rejections left the ranks of the Springfield companies much depleted and it was necessary to send officers to that city for recruits to fill the vacancies before the companies could be mustered in. Capt. Leonard of G, Lieut. Young of B and Lieut. Powers of K were sent on this duty and with them went about all of the men who had been rejected. As soon as the purpose of their visit was known in Springfield they were besieged by applicants for enlistment but having learned wisdom from what had happened in camp they took the precaution to have all the applicants pass a medical examination before bringing them to South Framingham and as a result few of the new men they brought down failed to pass the examining surgeons at the camp.

On May 6, another member of K company, Private Cook, was taken ill with tonsilitis and was sent home, much to his disgust.

On the same day the field and staff officers of the Second were mustered into the United States service by Lieut. E. M. Weaver, 2d artillery, who had been detailed as mustering officer for the Massachusetts volunteers. Adjutant Paul R. Hawkins was the first one to be mustered and he was followed by Quartermaster E. E. Sawtell. Surgeon Bowen and Assistant Surgeons Gates and Hitchcock had been mustered in on the day after our arrival in camp and had been assigned to duty in assisting in the examinations of recruits.

First Lieut. W. C. Hayes of G joined his company on the afternoon of the 6th and after being examined and accepted was assigned to duty.

On Saturday and Sunday, the 7th and 8th, three batches of additional recruits arrived in camp and were at once handed over to the examining surgeons. By Sunday K company had filled its ranks to the required number of 74 enlisted men and on that day was duly mustered into the military service of the United States for a period of two years "unless sooner discharged." The ceremony was a simple one. The company was marched over to brigade headquarters and formed in column of twos facing the mustering officer, Lieut. Weaver. The latter called out each man's name, beginning with the first sergeant and as each man answered he stepped to the front and facing about took position in front of the company in the same formation. The roll call over, the company was faced to the front, Lieut. Weaver removed his cap and the men uncovered. Then Lieut. Weaver read in impressive tones the oath of allegiance to the United States and administered it to the company, thus completing the ceremony which marked the transition of militiamen and raw recruits into soldiers of the United States. K company was the first company in Massachusetts to be mustered into the United States service and so far as known the first company in the country to be mustered in. That afternoon "government rations" were issued to K and the next day the men began eating them instead of the meals which had up to then been supplied by a caterer. Some of the men who failed to understand the difference between Uncle Sam's diet and that furnished at militia encampments found fault of course with the rations. Butter and milk are unknown in the regular soldiers' menu unless the company fund is drawn upon for them, and some of the men couldn't understand why they were not supplied and found fault accordingly. Later when we were all living luxuriously(?) in Cuba on "sowbelly" bacon, hardtack and coffee, sometimes without sugar, these men remembered with fond but unavailing regret the once despised government rations at

South Framingham. The fond parents and relatives who were told in letters from camp of how meager and unsatisfactory the first food furnished by Uncle Sam was may correct their idea by glancing over the rations issued for the first five days to K company while at South Framingham:

300 lbs. potatoes; 422 lbs. flour; 27¾ lbs. bacon; 7 lbs. rice; 43¾ lbs. beans; 30 lbs. coffee; 56¼ lbs. sugar; 15 lbs. salt; ¾ lb. pepper; 15 lbs. soap; 75 lbs. onions; 5¼ lbs. candles; 3¼ gallons vinegar and 422 lbs. fresh beef.

It is understood of course that the soap and candles were not issued as edibles but for cleansing and illuminating purposes. And it can also be seen that in the above rations there are possibilities for good eating and plenty of it. As a matter of fact milk and butter were soon supplied from the company funds.

G and B companies were mustered in on the 10th with full ranks. G was to have been mustered in the day previous but when the time arrived one private, a raw recruit, was missing and as the entire company was obliged to be on hand for muster the ceremony was dispensed with for that day and the men were marched back vowing vengeance upon the man who had kept them for 24 hours from getting into the service. Before very long another recruit was found and when the missing private turned up full of penitence and other things his uniform was taken off and after receiving a talking to from Capt. Leonard that made his cheeks burn with shame he was shipped out of camp.

The boys found plenty of amusement during their camp life and with nearly 1000 young fellows in one regiment time did not hang very heavily on their hands during the times between drills and other duties. Base ball and other sports were indulged in and letter writing and visits to the other regiments or an occasional pass to town prevented anything like ennui. In the Springfield companies there were few tent crews that did not have some distinctive appellation for their habitation. Private J. C. Ryan of B made his tent famous as a "steam laundry" and in G street there was the "Hotel Dingbat," so named because the men who occupied it could not think of anything else to call it. In K there was quickly organized an outfit later to be known as the "Wee Haws" and which made itself somewhat famous by the gift of song possessed by its members.

The "board of license commissioners" so famous during the encampment of 1897 was on hand but its members had but little of an official nature to do as the camp of '98 was officially a "dry camp." A good share of the dryness was, however, confined to the weather and a careful search of the records fails to show that any inmate of the camp died of thirst, although there were some serious cases.

CHAPTER V.

WE GET ORDERS TO LEAVE FOR THE SUNNY SOUTH AND OBEY THEM.

ALL of the time during our stay in camp speculation was rife as to when we were going to the front and how; also under what designation were we going. It had been circulated that we were to be known as the 63d United States Volunteers, and other rumors, all of which turned out to be just as near the truth as that one were put into commission. These marked the origin of the "Jo Jo" bureau of misinformation which later became an important feature of the campaign.

On the night of Wednesday, May 11th at 9.30, orders were flashed over the wires from Washington to Lieut. Weaver to send the Second at once to Tampa, Fla., where the army of invasion of Cuba was gathering. Almost everyone except the guard and a few officers and attaches at regimental headquarters, was asleep when the orders came but within a very few moments after their purport had been announced, there was the wildest scene of excitement in the camp that had ever been witnessed in South Framingham. From Lieut. Weaver the orders were quickly transmitted to regimental headquarters and from there to the officers of the regiment. Inside of ten minutes from their receipt by Lieut. Weaver, every man of the Second was awake and in his company street and exultant shouts that went up, quickly aroused the other regiments. The Second was to be the first command

Commissioned and Non-Commissioned Officers of G Company

from the old Bay State to be ordered outside her boundaries for active service and the men were so proud of it that they could not refrain from reminding the men of the other three regiments of the fact. To the credit of the latter it must be said that although at first they were a bit inclined to sulk because their regiment was not the first to be called upon, yet they soon realized that the honor was in a sense as much Massachusetts' as it was the Second's, and their cheers joined in with ours.

Meanwhile, the regimental and company officers were doing some lively work. Col. Clark had gone to Springfield that morning, and a number of officers and men were away on leave, no one expecting that the orders would come for a day or two. The regiment was ordered to move the next day and before the orders had been known of but a very few minutes, telegraph and telephone messages were sent to the absent ones informing them of what had happened. This done, the work of completing the equipment of the regiment was taken up and pushed in lively fashion. There were many little details to be attended to and there was little sleep for headquarters that night. How well the work was done is attested by the fact that at an early hour the next morning the regiment had its tents struck and packed, and long before the hour at which many of the folks at home were eating their breakfasts, was in readiness to move. Reveille was sounded at 4 o'clock that morning and by 6 there was but little remaining to be done.

Although anxious for active service there was one thing about the orders which was not at all relished by the regiment and that was the route to be followed. It had been expected and understood that when the Second would go south its route would be through Worcester and Springfield, thus giving us a chance for a genuine *au revoir* to home and friends. We all of us knew that the "farewell" accorded us on leaving Springfield for the camp at South Framingham would be tame indeed to the reception we might expect when we passed through there as United States Volunteers, with a large V, and bound for the front. Some of the boys, to be sure, dreaded the thought of having to say "good bye" to the accompaniment of tears and sobs again but the majority were anxious for one more look at what part of Springfield to be seen from the union station and were consequently much disappointed when it was announced that instead of going via Springfield, the route was to be by way of Newport, R. I.

There was much disappointment, too, in Springfield when the route was announced. But not to be be beaten, a party of citizens headed by Major H. S. Dickinson, arranged for a special train to South Framingham, the day we were to leave and so we were not allowed to go without some sort of a farewell demonstration from the people of our own city.

On the day previous to our receiving the "rush" orders to the south, a number of visitors including ex-Lieut. Gov. W. H. Haile, Col. A. H. Goetting and James D. Gill of Springfield were in camp, and it came to their attention that the Second was not provided with a band or even field music. No regimental bands were included in the organization of the volunteer regiments nor even field music, the sole musical property being the bugles of which there were two to each company. It was looked upon as a proper and desirable thing that the Second should at least have field music, or in civilian parlance, a drum corps, and these three gentlemen constituted themselves a committee on ways and means to that end. It was known that there were enough musicians in the regiment to form a drum corps if there were instruments provided for them and before the next day through the generosity of the three gentlemen named, the Second was provided with fifes, drums, etc., and the members of the corps selected.

Thursday, May 12th, we bade good-bye to South Framingham. There was difficulty in getting transportation for our baggage and it was not until a late hour in the afternoon that everybody was in readiness. Meanwhile we hung around our former quarters and killed time as best we could. A short time after dinner, our last meal on the "old camp ground," the "assembly" and "adjutant's call" were sounded and the regiment was formed to pass in review before Gov. Wolcott. The march past over, hollow square was formed and the governor presented the officers their commissions and made a brief speech telling us to uphold the honor of the old commonwealth.

While this was going on we heard the strains of a band and soon in marched a delegation from Springfield, headed by the Second regiment band and led by Mayor Dickinson, members of Wilcox post of the Grand Army and Peabody Guard Veterans, while relatives and friends of the boys made up the rest of the 500 in the party. Soon after their arrival we were dismissed and then followed one of the interesting scenes of our war experience. Hardly had we broken ranks before we were surrounded by the visitors and there was falling upon each other's necks, handshaking, good wishes, smiles and tears all commingled in one scene of such excitement as we had never been through before. Every male visitor brought cigars or refreshments for the boys and for an hour or so nothing was too good for us.

But all things have an end and finally the bugles blew and after a last hurried kiss or handshake we fell in again and marched out to the parade ground for the last time. The colors dipped once more to the governor and then through a double line of cheering soldiers from the other regiments and our own friends we marched out of the camp and down the dusty road to the railroad station, escorted by two troops of cavalry and amid the cheers and good wishes of the thousands who thronged the walks. We passed under the handsome arch erected by the people of South

Framingham in honor of the soldiers and after one last opportunity to say farewell went on board the special trains waiting for us. So we left good old Massachusetts.

On our way to Newport we were shown how the people of other places regarded us. At every station our train passed through there were cheering crowds and enthusiasm seemed to be in evidence everywhere. We reached Newport about 9.30 and were transferred to the palatial steamer "Pilgrim" of the Fall River line.

"This isn't so bad for army travelling," was the common remark as soon as the boys found what accommodations had been made for them. There were nearly enough staterooms to provide every man with a bunk and those who failed to get a room found nice, thick mattresses spread for them on the saloon floors. It brought the "Trip to New York" and Valiquet back to the memories of many of us because the accommodations were so different.

But it was a tired lot of boys that boarded the Pilgrim that night and it was not long before all of them were testing the mattresses and bunks, after indulging by the way for the first time in the "travel ration." This was our first encounter with the canned beef department but somehow it tasted better then than it ever did afterwards. Also we allowed our teeth to play with the ligneous hardtack and finally fatigued with our exertions we slept soundly.

The next morning when we woke up we were in the East river and at the sight of her blue coated cargo every steam craft that met the Pilgrim saluted with steam whistles while their crews or passengers as well as those of the sailing craft cheered and waved handkerchiefs or anything else waveable. From every factory along the shore came the shrieks of the steam whistles and the shouts of their occupants and our progress down the river to the Fall River line pier was a triumphal progress.

When we reached the pier it was not long before we were

transferred to the transports Saratoga and Vigilancia, the Springfield companies being on board the latter. Then it was that we began to realize what war was. Down in the dirty, dark and ill smelling hold we could see men at work building rough wooden bunks for us and the language used concerning these bunks and their location was copious and picturesque to a high degree. No "Pilgrim" accommodations were these. No mattresses 12 inches thick to rest our weary bones upon but the soft and splintered pine boards were to form our couch. Also the travel ration with its components of canned roast beef(?), canned corn beef, canned beans and hardtack was beginning to pall upon our palates. We were not used to such Epicurean fare and began to fear gout and other incidentals of too luxurious living. So we gathered together and said things but all the time the carpenters went on constructing the bunks and no dinners were brought on for us from the Waldorf-Astoria.

Our first cruise on the Vigilancia was further up the North river where we waited until late in the afternoon and while waiting many of the boys managed to get ashore. Some of them were nearly left behind as we pulled out of the dock and a few did get left on shore, but they chartered a tug and soon caught us. That night our transports sailed down the harbor as far as Bedloe's Island where we anchored opposite the Bartholdi statue and where we stayed anchored until the next afternoon. That night the much discussed wooden troughs officially named bunks were used and were the cause of much profane language for which the recording angel ought to be able to find a good excuse if he has any love for volunteer soldiers in his composition. Late that afternoon we were taken over to Jersey City and transferred to a special train of three sections of 14 cars each on which we were to make the trip to Tampa. And thus ended our first sea voyage.

CHAPTER VI.

WE GO TO THE SOUTHLAND AND BEGIN TO FIND OUT WHERE WE ARE AT.

ON Saturday evening, May 14, we started once more for the South, this time by train and had the distinguished honor of beating out the much-advertised 71st New York, which had been ordered to start at the same time, but forgot its tentage on board the steamers and was obliged to wait for several hours in consequence. Our train accommodations could have been much worse, the train being run in three sections of 14 cars each and as four companies travelled on each section this arrangement gave each company three cars, while a sleeping car was reserved for the officers and with a baggage car made up the section. With three cars to a company there was plenty of room for the men and we managed to sleep quite comfortably. At every station along the route we received plenty of greetings and this happened so frequently after we got below Mason & Dixon's line that the boys wondered a little, inasmuch as we were from "Black Massachusetts." But it was evident that all but a very few of the people of the South realized that the civil war was over and we got no heartier reception anywhere along the route than in Virginia and North and South Carolina.

We reached Washington early Sunday morning and made a brief stop just long enough to allow some of the boys to make a raid on a couple of milk wagons. To our disappointment the train did not run through the city but skirted it and we failed to get a glimpse of any of the show places. We kept on going and late Monday evening, the 16th, landed at Lakeland, Fla., where we went into camp, our destination having been changed by telegraphic orders received soon after crossing the Florida line.

Life on the train was not very exciting. We made but few stops and those mainly to change engines. In South Carolina we made our first acquaintance with wood burning engines. After these were hitched on it was a case of stopping every few miles to "wood up." When the train did not stop for wood it did for water and between them both progress was slow to us but we found that according to southern ideas we were going at express speed.

Our troop train was a great attraction for the children at the stations where we stopped and it was a common thing for the boys and girls of these places to hand us bunches of jessamine and magnolia flowers while the older folk looked on approvingly. The colored people were somewhat demonstrative but both they and the white folks never neglected an opportunity to sell us cakes and pies at every stop. The pies reminded us of those we had been getting at home, they were so different, but as a relief from canned meat and beans they were welcome. Occasionally when we stopped we found it possible to purchase bottled beer of an inferior grade, but better than most of the water we had to drink.

On the trip south Lieuts. Young and Vesper of B company established records as sleepers that put them far ahead in their class. Captains Leonard and McDonald had the same section in the sleeping car and about every night there could be heard a more or less vigorous protest from the former against Capt. McDonald's use of a 700 horse power pipe. Lieut. Harry Parkhurst of K was the victim of much "jollying" over a story printed in a New York newspaper to the effect that he was a nephew of the Rev. Dr. Parkhurst of New York, but he took it good naturedly.

At Dupont, Ga., Private William Ferrier of G foraged a little during a brief stop and captured a diminutive specimen of the "razor back" hog prevalent in that locality and bore him in triumph to the train. Any visions of pork chops which might have been indulged in were dispelled by a look at the pig's anatomy which was plainly visible through his skin but he was taken along just the same and met his fate at Lakeland when he was killed and roasted by Private "Dido" Hunt of G and served up to a small but select circle.

At one of the many stops in Florida a portly colored lady hung about the train and made violent love to the good looking officers, her comments on the personal appearance of some of them being rather more pungent than flattering. So far as known she did not steal any of them.

During the stay at South Framingham Privates E. N. Aiken and B. R. Madison of K company had blossomed out as composers and one of their effusions which was sung by the more or less able musicians of the company in camp and on the train to the tune of: "There'll be a Hot Time in the Old Town To-night" was as follows:

"When you hear those guns go bang, bang, bang,
We'll all join in and lick that Dago gang,
For we want war or we'll have no name at all,
There'll be a hot time when the bugle shall call."

The above was Private Aiken's. Here is Private Madison's:

"In the battle front we stand with our rifles in our hand
And for Cuba's freedom we will ever fight;
And with showers of shot and shell,
We'll send the Spaniards straight to h——l,
When we march into Havana bye and bye.

CHORUS.

Tramp, tramp, tramp the boys are marching,
Cheer up, Cuba, we will come,
And beneath the starry flag
We'll tear down the Spanish rag
And float the Cuban flag forevermore."

Our arrival at Lakeland was marked by an incident which went to show that we were not in the north. Just as our train pulled in a shooting affray, in which a couple of troopers from the Tenth U. S. cavalry, a colored regiment and some white people participated, occurred and a white citizen of the town was killed. As nearly as we could understand it the troopers were not to blame but shot in self defense but there was much excitement in the town and strong patrols of the First U. S. cavalry, a white regiment, were sent out. We were kept in the train that night and the next morning after a bath in one of the many lakes from which the town takes its name, marched to our camp at the fair grounds and on the shores of Lake Morton. The camp was pitched on an elevation and under the southern pine and cypress trees from which hung long festoons of Spanish moss. Much of this was gathered for bedding but it was soon abandoned for this purpose when it was found that it harbored numbers of lizards and sometimes small snakes.

Our neighbors at the camp were the First and Tenth regular cavalry and the 71st New York which arrived a day after we did. The 71st men being from Manhattan were inclined to be a bit fresh at first but they soon came to understand that the Second was not exactly a "farmer" regiment and let us alone. One disagreeable incident went to show that among the New York officers were some snobs. Sergeant James Gibbons of G while "down town" one day went into the dining room of the hotel and ordered his dinner. The commanding officer of the 71st and some of his officers were in the room at the time and as soon as he realized that an enlisted man was actually daring to eat in the same room with him his indignation became so great that he walked over to the table where Sergeant Gibbons was seated and ordered him to leave the place, saying that only officers were allowed in the dining room. Sergeant Gibbons did not feel like moving and the hotel proprietor assured him that he would be served as well as any officer. So he refused to budge and enjoyed his dinner, much to the disgust of the New York officer.

Life at Lakeland was fairly enjoyable. The temperature was high, ranging from 84 on one day it rained to 124 on a day it did not. We had our big wall tents we had brought with us from South Framingham and soon had them filled with more or less crude devices in the way of furniture. Mattresses there were none and our beds were Mother Earth which was of a brunette hue down there. Bathing in the lake was a favorite pastime between drills but after the muddy bottom had been stirred up a little it was a question whether we were dirtier before the bath or after it. There were all kinds of "Jo Jos" about a huge alligator who made his home in the lake but he had evidently heard of our appetites and kept out of sight.

The First cavalry, camped some distance on our right, had established a canteen soon after its arrival and it became a favorite place for our boys. A couple of days after our arrival we got our first mail from home and that day was a red letter one in our Lakeland life.

Just before reaching Lakeland some K company foragers had captured a goat at one of the stops but the owner pursued the animal to Lakeland and when he put in a claim for him Capt. Warriner ordered the "billy" given up. Our menu in camp was far more varied than on the train for "post" rations were being issued and the company cooks were "getting on to their jobs." Private Mandeville, who afterwards acquired much fame by being left behind at Fort Tampa, presided over the kitchen of G. In B company Walter Butler got up savory dishes and Private Harry Fisher looked after the culinary department for K. Butter was conspicuous by its absence from the table and one boy in K missed it so much that he dreamed of it. One night his dreams were so realistic that his cry of "Ma, please pass the butter," awoke his tent mates and that expression was the rallying cry in K for several days.

The death of Private Weslie Brass of Westfield, a member of I company, cast a gloom over the regiment and all the companies turned out to do escort duty when the body was shipped home. His was the first death in the regiment.

On Sunday, May 30th, orders came to break camp the following day and proceed to Tampa, which we did, arriving there on Monday afternoon, the 31st.

CHAPTER VII.

WE STAY IN YBOR CITY AND THEN ENJOY (?) LIFE ON TRANSPORTS IN THE HARBOR.

OUR stay in Tampa lasted from May 31st to June 7th and it was not wholly unenjoyable. In some respects the place was better than Lakeland, but we felt the heat far more than was the case in that town and the camp location was not as good as that of our camp there. But we were near Tampa and there were many opportunities for us to get to the city, our camp being in one of the suburbs some three miles from Tampa and known as Ybor City. Its population was made up mainly of Cubans and negroes and a number of cigar factories were located there. The Cubans were all "patriots" of course, but our disenchantment as to Cuban patriots had already begun and we paid them little attention. On our right was camped a battalion of the Fourth regular artillery (heavy) and this was probably the occasion of a rumor which had persistent circulation for several days that we were to be transformed from infantry to a heavy artillery regiment and assigned to sea coast duty.

We had a lovely time pitching our tents and making camp. Owing to a delay in laying out the camp it was not until after dark on the day of our arrival that we set to work to pitch our tents and as a result it was not only late before we got to sleep but the next morning considerable work had to be done in rectifying the alignment of the company streets. The soil was nice white sand which made fairly good beds.

On the afternoon of the next day we found out what a Florida "shower" could do when it tried. The rain came on unexpectedly and within a very few moments everything was in a flood. But few of the boys had taken the precaution to dig trenches around their tents and after the rain began to come down in sheets they were compelled to get out in it and dig or else have their quarters flooded. Here was where the value of the rubber blankets issued to us at South Framingham was shown.

It was while we were at Ybor City that our regiment was definitely assigned. We were put into the First Brigade of the Second Division of the Fifth army corps, our brigade commander being temporarily Col. Van Horn of the 22nd infantry while Gen. H. W. Lawton was in command of the division. This set at rest all the rumors about our being heavy artillery, cavalry and several other things. It also meant that we were to go to Cuba among the very first of the invading troops and there was no end of enthusiasm when this was understood.

During our stay in Ybor City Wagoners Kingston of B, Shene of G and Boule of K became expert drivers of the army mule wagon although their trials with the mule were many and various. In B street there were some pathetic scenes when the members of the Kanewah club got together and talked over how nice it would be "to be there" even if the gasoline stove did not always work.

Pay day came June 4th and we got our first "whack" at Uncle Sam's good money. It was welcome, for since leaving South Framingham but little had been in circulation among our boys and we gave the paymaster the "glad hand." In return, he lined us up by companies and gave us greenbacks and a little silver. We had expected a full month's pay but were disappointed, our pay being calculated from

May 3d, the day we had officially been mustered in, to the first of June. There were many applications for passes to visit Tampa that day and the majority of them were granted. The Seminole hotel and the stores in Ybor City and Tampa did a rushing business that afternoon and evening.

The "Wee Haws" of K contributed not a little to the gaiety of our camp life at this time and one of their songs to the air of "Rally 'Round the Flag" and reflecting upon the subsistence department was popular. It went like this:

> Down with the hardtack!
>   Hurrah, boys, hurrah,
> Down with the canned beef;
>   We wonder what you are;
> For we'll rally 'round the beans, boys,
>   We'll rally once again
> Shouting the battle cry of "Wee Haw."
>
> 'Please pass the butter,'
>   Hurrah, boys, hurrah!
> If the coffee was much thicker
>   We'd sell it off for tar;
> For we'll never look like Billy Fish
>   Unless we get more grub—
> Shouting the battle cry of "Wee Haw."
>
> Ade Potter's growing thinner,
>   Healey's just the same
> Brazzil, Breck and Nesbitt swear,
>   Their biscuit box is lame;
> For George Potter ate his canteen
>   And Aiken ate the strap
> And McCullough shouts the battle cry of "Wee Haw!"

About this time some brainless individual sent alarming news home in a letter, which was published in the Springfield newspapers, to the effect that sickness was prevalent in our camp and that a large proportion of the men of the three companies from that city were in the hospital seriously ill. As a result we soon began to get letters of anxious inquiry from the folks at home, and it was some time before we could fully reassure them that the reports had been extremely exaggerated and that there was but little illness and none of a serious nature in our ranks.

While in Ybor City we lost two men, Privates Luther of K and Monteverde of G. Both were ordered to be discharged from the service, because of having enlisted while under age and without the consent of their parents or guardians. Monteverde was reluctant to leave the regiment and pleaded hard to be allowed to go with us to Cuba even as a civilian employe, and when that was refused he offered to go without any pay. But this was found to be impossible and he and Luther were obliged to return home. The case of Private John K. DeLoach of B company was a hard one. He had enlisted in South Framingham and in some way his relatives, who resided in Atlanta, Ga., heard of it, and as he was under age and had not their consent, applied for his discharge. Orders to have him discharged were issued but they failed to arrive while we were in Tampa, and did not reach us until after the regiment had landed in Cuba and done its share in capturing Santiago. DeLoach had done his duty during the most arduous part of the campaign, and as a result was given a "bob tail" discharge and left to get back to the United States as best he could. Sometimes the rewards of patriotism are not great, and this was certainly one of the instances.

June 6th orders were received to break camp and proceed to Port Tampa, there to go on board the transports for Cuba. We broke camp all right, got our tents down and all baggage packed and saw them sent away and then proceeded to wait. We waited all that afternoon and night and until late in the afternoon of the next day before our belated transportation was arranged for. As a result of a blunder in the quartermaster's department, we were compelled to bivouac that night without any shelter. This was our first real acquaintance with the fact expressed in the statement attributed to Gen. Sherman, that "War is h—l."

Late in the afternoon of June 7th, we marched to the railroad and went on board a train which after a couple of hours brought us to Port Tampa, distance about eight miles. Here we found some practical illustrations of the beautiful manner in which the quartermaster's department was working. It had been stated to Col. Clark that on arriving at Port Tampa we were to immediately go on board the transports, but after disembarking from the train and waiting for some time it was found that no transports had been assigned to us. Nothing could be done in the matter that night, and we were to be left to shift for ourselves as best we could. There were no barracks in Port Tampa, and it was too late to go into camp even if we had our tentage with us, which we did not. After considerable scouting, Col. Clark discovered that quarters might be found in the freight sheds on a long pier, and we started for them only to have the entire regiment halted and held up for some minutes at the point of the bayonet of a sentinel of the First Illinois regiment, who was on guard at the entrance to the pier and had orders to let no one pass. This obstacle was finally surmounted and we marched onto the pier and made ourselves comfortable as best we could.

During that night on the pier the foraging instincts of Private "Dido" Hunt of G company became active, and as a result he and several members of that company passed the long hours of the night very comfortably. The freight sheds were divided into sections, and in that allowed to G was a lot of freight. Included were two innocent looking barrels, but guided solely by instinct "Dido" decided to investigate their contents. With this end in view he spread his roll and blanket by the side of the barrels, and, lying on his side began to cut a hole through the staves of one of them. This was rather difficult because of the sentries, but it was finally accomplished, and much to the forager's intense satisfaction, the

insertion of his hand through the hole and into the barrel, revealed to him that it was filled with bottled beer. Satisfying himself in the only proper manner, that there was no mistake, he acquainted the members of his squad and a few others with his find and soon an impromptu picnic was in progress. Under the very noses of the sentries, the contents of that barrel of beer disappeared before morning, and to those in the secret the night passed very pleasantly.

The next morning four companies and headquarters of the Second were transferred to the transport Orizaba, the companies being G, B, K and D. The transport already had on board the Eighth and Twenty-second regular infantry, and as a result our boys were crowded about on the decks and compelled to sleep anywhere they could. The officers were crowded into the staterooms and their experiences on the Orizaba were not much more enjoyable than those of the men. Some of the regulars, with a fine contempt for volunteers, did their best to make things as unpleasant for us as possible, but the majority were of a different disposition and aided us all they could, which unfortunately was not much.

We expected to sail that day but did not. The same could be said about our expectations and disappointments every succeeding day until we did finally sail on the 14th. Before that happened we were again transferred, this time to the well remembered transport, Knickerbocker. This event happened on the 13th and when we found that the Knickerbocker's number was 13, that she had that number of letters in her name and that about everybody and everything connected with her was more or less mixed up with the alleged unlucky number some of us began to wonder what would happen. Fortunately nothing did, but that was because somebody, not connected with the war department, or with this world, was looking after us. The third battalion was added to our force on board the Knickerbocker, the second being on the Seneca and the Manteo.

On the evening of the 13th the 13 hoodoo began to work. A steam pipe burst and some of the boys, thinking a general explosion would follow, jumped from the deck to the dock, but although there was considerable fuss and excitement no one was hurt. That night sleep on the Knickerbocker was out of the question, for a gang of negro roustabouts was engaged all night in loading provisions onto our steamer and their cries, together with the noise of the steam winches prevented any sleep. On the afternoon of the next day, the 14th, the steamer finally cast off and started down the harbor in the wake of the other transports. After being tied up in Tampa harbor for six long days we were at last at sea and bound for Cuba.

CHAPTER VIII.

WE HAVE A LOVELY SAIL ON THE PALATIAL KNICKERBOCKER AND REACH CUBA WITHOUT MISHAP.

OUR voyage to Cuba on Transport No. 13, unofficially known as the Knickerbocker, will long linger in our memories. The Knickerbocker was a lovely ship but her loveliness was of such a nature that it was seldom referred to without a free and unlimited use of adjectives in the ratio of more than 16 to 1. After a while it got to be a case of "Don't speak of her past, boys," and we seldom did. The present was bad enough and as for her future, all of us had grave doubts concerning it. There was a story from apparently authentic sources, that before the government, in a moment of temporary aberation, engaged the services of the Knickerbocker as a transport, she had been engaged in conveying Italian emigrants from New York to New Orleans, and her interior condition when we boarded her gave conformation of the stories.

Many words could be written concerning the Knickerbocker and our opinion of her, but as a good share of them would form language not generally used in the best society, it will be perhaps as well to draw the veil of silence over a good part of it.

Her captain's name was Betts and he was an aged individual who savored much of the sea and who evidently had been the victim of an early or late disappointment, either in love or something else, that resulted in souring him towards himself and everybody else. The name of the steward of the boat is unknown, but this did not bother the boys much, their usual designation of him being "thief" or "robber" or any term of opprobrium that came handy. If he was a poor man when the Knickerbocker sailed with us from Tampa harbor, there was no reason why he could not have returned with money enough to start a fair sized bank account, for he sold us everything there was to sell, and considerable that he had no right to, and he always charged us Klondike prices for everything. He was never under suspicion of giving away anything, not even himself. Before the voyage was half over there came near being a mutiny among the crew which had discovered, so they said, that the steward was taking the provisions destined for them and selling them to such of our boys as had money and had become weary of the luxurious and varied fare given us by the government. At the same time his extortions had become so burdensome to our boys that muttered threats against him were heard and but for some of the cooler heads among the soldiers he might have been the victim of the vengeance both of the crew and the troops.

There were thirteen staterooms on the boat and into these were crowded 32 officers. The men were "bunked" in the hold, and if there was any provision for ventilation other than the hatches, no trace was ever found of it. On the first night out the men slept on the decks and so were enabled to pass the night in considerable comfort, for if the deck planks were hard, there was at least some air and the cool sea breeze made sleeping possible. But on the second night out there came trouble. The surgeon was fearful that the night dews would have a bad effect on the men, and had been told so much of the evil effects of sleeping out in the air in tropical latitudes that he believed it best for the men to sleep below decks. He pressed his views upon the commanding officer, and the result was an order to the officer of the day to allow no men to sleep above decks on that or the succeeding nights of the voyage.

Naturally, when this order was communicated to the men, there was a protest. There was a decided difference of opinion between the men and the surgeon as to the evil results from sleeping on deck, and the men were inclined to rebel against the order. However, Capt. McDonald of B company was officer of the day, and no matter what his sympathies were, orders were orders. So soon after "taps" had sounded he and the guard made a tour of the boat and the sleepers were informed that they must retire to the bunks below and complete their slumbers. Then there was a howl of remonstrance, but it was without avail. The sleepers were rounded up and hustled below. In protest against this came all sorts of noise from the sleeping quarters. Songs and yells, and there was much satire in many of the songs, came up from below. The surgeons were alluded to as "Horse doctors" and "Salts," and one chorus that came floating up through the hatches ran something like this:

"What do they give us for stomach ache?"
"Salts."
"What do they give us for a broken leg?"
"Salts."
"What do they give us for rheumatism?"
"Salts."

And so on through a catalogue of all the various diseases incident to man or animals.

Finally the noise became so great that Capt. McDonald threatened to have the hatches closed, thus destroying the last faint chance of obtaining any air. This was met by the threat that if the hatches were closed bullets would be fired through them, but after a while the noise quieted down and the men dropped off to sleep. After that night the order to sleep below decks was pretty well obeyed as the reason for it begun to be understood by the men and they realized that it was prompted by a desire for their welfare and not to annoy them.

Not all the boys slept below, however. Emery, Morehouse and Kelly of K had managed to secrete themselves in one of the ships boats and made it their sleeping quarters all the time of the voyage. As it was covered by a tarpaulin they were well protected from the dews or rains, and in any case they managed to keep the secret so well that they were not molested.

G company suffered a terrible loss on the day we sailed. Private Mandeville, the company cook, had managed to cut himself so badly in the arm with a carving knife, during our stay at Lakeland, that he had been excused from that duty. On our last day at Port Tampa he had obtained shore leave and utillized it so well in looking at the wine when it was red, or something that had the same effect, that he was in a trance when the orders came to leave. So when the Knickerbocker sailed, G was one man short, and after the requisite ten days had elapsed Private Mandeville was put on the rolls as a deserter. Fortunately for him, it was established on our return that he was not technically a deserter, it appearing that when he woke up he had reported himself to an officer in Tampa, and had been assigned to remain with a party of the 71st New York which had likewise been left behind.

Of mascots there were many on board. First of all came one James Sargent of Washington, D. C., a young colored lad better known as "Snowball." He had come on from Washington with some District of Columbia troops and finding that they were not going immediately to Cuba or for some other reason he got on board the Knickerbocker and attached himself for better or worse to the Second Massachusetts. Any member of the regiment can answer the query as to whether it was for better or worse for the Second.

Then there were James and Willie Turner, two young

white boys from Tampa who had an uncontrollable desire to hie themselves over the seas to Cuba and there end the lives of more or less Spaniards. They remained with us until the landing on the island and then divorced themselves from the Second and attached themselves to two regular regiments. Both stood the campaign in far better shape than the older men and returned to this country with enlarged views and a determination to enlist in the regulars as soon as they were of the requisite age.

G company had two mascots in "Rations" and "Hardtack," dogs of the cur variety. Rations did not last out the voyage, her career being cut short by some miscreant who threw her overboard one night, much to the indignation of the men of the company.

A predominating feature of the trip across was the excellent fare provided for the enlisted men by a thoughtful government. Life at sea on a steady diet of canned beef, canned beans and canned tomatoes, hardtack and ship's water is not conducive to embonpoint or a cheerful and contented disposition. In the hurry of fitting up the Knickerbocker as a transport no provision had been made to do any cooking for the men, even if there had been anything to cook, and there was not even a place where coffee, of which we had plenty, could be made. Finally after a couple of days out some vigorous "kicking" resulted in the company cooks being grudgingly allowed the use of the galley for coffee making purposes but with the poor water the coffee was hardly equal to that furnished at Delmonico's or other places where most of us had been in the habit of eating.

As to the water an entire chapter could not do justice to its qualities. There were two brands on board, one being Mississippi river fluid with an equal quantity of mud of a rich brown color in suspension. After obtaining a cupful of this mixture it was necessary to allow it to stand for some little time in order that the mud might settle to the bottom.

With all its faults, however, this water when strained was sweet and drinking it did not cause remorse.

The other water had been obtained in Tampa and it was called water principally because it was contained in the water tanks. It did not look much like water and tasted still less like it. But that and the muddy fluid was all there was to drink and we had to make the best of it.

One day when the canned beef was even worse than usual and the canned beans greasier than ever there came to the vision of certain members of the Springfield companies, who happened to be looking through the skylight into the steward's pantry, a delicious looking piece of cold roast beef hanging peacefully from a hook and destined for the officers' lunch. Constant looking at that well cooked piece of fresh beef begot longing, then covetousness and desire. By a silent but unanimous vote it was decided that such a nice piece of beef would be better appreciated by hungry enlisted men than by the officers who had been getting more or less of it, at their own expense, during the voyage and the next thing was the informal appointment of a committee on ways and means to procure the aforesaid beef. An examination revealed that the skylight could be opened from the deck and further that a boathook was handy. These facts ascertained, a watch was kept until the occupant of the pantry had gone out for a moment, the skylight was quickly opened, the boathook manipulated and the piece of beef lifted to the deck. The cook re-entered the pantry just as the beef was disappearing through the skylight and the expression on his face haunted the participants in the "Disappearing beef mystery" for many hours.

In one corner of the upper deck that afternoon were a number of men upon whose faces rested an expression of perfect contentment and whose hands could occasionally be seen to wander over their stomachs as if to assure themselves that cold roast beef was a suitable article of diet for a voyage in

the tropics. As no ill effects were recorded the question was settled satisfactorily to them but it is also on record that no more tempting bits were hung within reach of open skylights or wandering boathooks. It is also a matter of history that the officers' lunch that day was rather a poor meal and there was no cold meat on the table. But Bates didn't care.

How the Knickerbocker ever escaped being run down or colliding with some other of the vessels of the fleet is one of the mysteries of the deep. Not less than half a dozen narrow escapes are on record in the memory of the men who were on her and on one or two occasions the escapes were so narrow that a few feet either way would have done the job for the Knickerbocker and her crew and passengers. On one occasion another boat came so near to running us down that half the men were ready to jump into the sea but the other boat finally sheered off by the closest margin. The "Thirteen" hoodoo came near to finding believers among those on the Knickerbocker before Cuba was reached.

Bathing hours were established on board after the first day out, each company being allowed an hour aft each day during which the men could "turn the hose" on each other to their heart's content. As, however, there was but little salt water soap on board and that little was in the hands of the steward to be retailed by him at robber baron prices these attempts at cleanliness proved rather abortive, for it was soon ascertained that ordinary soap does not lather in salt water and the effects of the bath under these circumstances was worse if anything than in Lakeland.

So the days went on until on the 20th we saw the low outline of the Cuban coast late in the afternoon and at the same time saw the flashes and heard the dull reports of big guns which told us that the navy was having a brush with the foe. It lasted only for a few moments, but this was the first time we had heard guns fired in actual conflict and although we could see but little the rigging was crowded until long after the guns were silent. We learned afterwards that it was only a little brush some of the blockading fleet were having with a fort near Santiago but it was mighty interesting to us while it lasted. All the next day the fleet cruised about apparently aimlessly and that night the Knickerbocker "got lost." How it ever happened no one knows excepting the captain of the ship and he never volunteered an explanation so far as we knew. It was expected that we would land that day but just before dusk a dispatch boat raced up alongside and without stopping speed an officer on board shouted through a megaphone an order to Captain Betts to continue "cruising to the northwest, keeping in touch with the fleet.' So off we cruised to the northwest but the rest of the order as to keeping in touch with the fleet was not carried out. The next morning when we woke up we found the Knickerbocker all alone with not a sail or line of smoke on the horizon and with apparently no one knowing where we were or what we were doing there. Inquiries of Captain Betts met with gruff and non-committal response and it was not until just before noon that we came in sight of the rest of the fleet off Daiquiri and learned that the landing had begun and that had we got there when we should the Second would have been the first regiment to land on Cuban soil. Then things were said concerning Capt. Betts and his boat that would not look nice in print.

Over on our left the big guns of the warships were pounding away at the fortifications while the small caliber guns were sending in a storm of bullets into the woods and hills along the shore, clearing them out before the landing. From the warships to the transports danced an almost steady stream of launches and small boats to assist in the landing. The invasion of Cuba by the Fifth army corps was a fact at last.

CHAPTER IX.

WHEREIN IS NARRATED OUR LANDING AT DAIQUIRI AND SOME THINGS WHICH SUBSEQUENTLY HAPPENED.

IT was not until well along in the afternoon that the Knickerbocker's passengers started for the shore and as it was not all of them landed that day, the third battalion being left on board until the 23d.

For many long hours the steamer backed and filled together with the other vessels and the men, loaded down as they were with their field equipment and waiting for the word to disembark, found plenty of time to enjoy the stirring scenes about them. There were the grim painted war ships, all ready for business and their hustling "Jackies" working like beavers to aid in landing us "doughboys." Between the big ships danced the saucy torpedo boats and destroyers and quick puffing launches having in tow strings of small boats, these being our means of transportation from the ship to the land. In front were the frowning hills which guarded the coast line and from which an enemy of any determination could have easily prevented our landing. On a plateau directly in front of us was the village of Daiquiri, abandoned that morning by the Spaniards after a brief bombardment by our fleet, while a force of Cubans got along in time to worry the retreating enemy. A portion of the village and the works were still smoldering, having been fired by the Spaniards before they left the place.

Daiquiri was the seat of the Spanish-American Iron company and a narrow guage railroad connects it with Juguaracito or Siboney where the company had quite an extensive establishment. Jutting out into the water was a high iron pier and it was supposed we were to land there, but this was found to be impossible after one or two trials.

Meanwhile after long waiting a dinky little steam launch from the battleship Massachusetts and followed by a string of small boats, came alongside the Knickerbocker and the youthful ensign in charge allowed that he was ordered to take headquarters and as many others of the regiment as possible on shore. This was agreeable and Col. Clark and his field and staff embarked in the launch without much trouble, although the job of climbing down a slippery rope ladder, then hanging on by both hands to the side ropes and waiting until the next high wave brought the launch up to within a couple of feet of you and then falling more or less, mostly less, gracefully into it, was not particularly pleasing. After headquarters, a platoon of G company embarked and this filled the boats.

How to get on shore from the boats appeared to grow into a serious problem as we neared the landing place. This was an old wooden pier, which jutted out some little distance from the land. There was a heavy surf on and the little basin in which the pier stood was jammed with boats and launches, all apparently very much snarled up but which in reality were being ably managed. After much maneuvering our launch was jammed alongside the pier and the next problem was how to get upon it. The supporting piles rose high up from the water and their slimy surface offered no inducement to attempt climbing. One moment we would be down in the trough of a wave and then the launch would be lifted up almost to the top of the pier and the sailors would be hard put to it to keep the boats from being dashed against the huge piling of the pier. The method of our landing could hardly be called dignified. As the boat would be raised almost to a level with the floor of the pier by a wave our rolls and equipment would be tossed up to some soldiers waiting to assist us. Then down the boat would go again and when the next wave raised it we would stand up on the thwarts of the boat, reach up our hands, two of the men on the pier would grasp them and we would scramble up the best we could. In this way the first lot was landed and the boats hustled back to the ship after another load of passengers. The pier was connected with the land by some loose planks and across these we walked gingerly, finally reaching terra firma. We were on Cuban soil at last.

On shore there was as much bustle and confusion as in the landing. Many of the regulars and a part of "Ours" had already landed but there appeared to be no system, and officers and men were scattered about everywhere. A short distance from the pier was a typical Cuban "shack" as the regulars called it, a roughly built shed with a roof of palm leaf thatch and around this was a lot of Cuban soldiers who were making themselves "good fellows" by giving away cocoanuts, of which they had a couple of large bags. They, the soldiers, were of varying shades of blackness and their "uniforms" consisted mostly of nothing. Some had more clothing than the others, but few had anything like a complete outfit. They were barefooted and bareheaded but all had the inevitable machete and some kind of a firearm, from the latest model Spanish mauser and the navy Lee to an old shotgun. They could talk English about as well as we could Spanish and the sign language was used with more or less success.

Having filled up on cocoanuts, which tasted good, we became thirsty. A water pipe ran along the ground and we soon found a faucet, but the first man to take a drink spat out the water and said some sharp and emphatic things concerning it at which we mildly wondered until he calmed down sufficiently to tell us that it was "hot enough to boil eggs in." Sure enough it was. The pipes ran along on the surface of the ground and the sun did the rest.

"*Mucho caliente agua,*" commented a ragged "Cubana" as he noticed our disgusted looks and one or two who understood enough Spanish to know what he meant agreed with him. Then he grinned as only a Cuban can and pointing to the plateau where the main part of the village was located, said: "*Agua fresca,*" which being interpreted meant "cold water." So off we started for the plateau and there found several barrels of fresh water which was fairly cool. Among the "shacks" which composed the town we found a "brigade" of the "brave" Cuban soldiers. They were having a good time recounting their exploits and staring at "*los Americano soldados,*" whose rough and ready manners were not always to their liking. A few of their field officers were almost white in color and decently uniformed but the majority, like the men, were black and distinguished from their men by small silver stars worn on a strap across the breast, three being the insignia of a captain, two of a first lieutenant and one of a second lieutenant.

A point of much interest to our men were the burning shops, which the Spaniards had fired before retreating. On the railway track was a locomotive and some cars which had been disabled and burnt. Additional interest was caused by the pursuit, capture and summary execution of an unwise pig by a mob of our men and Cubans.

All our battalions having landed, we began our march into the interior just before 5 o'clock. The brigade commander, Col. Van Horn of the 22d was injured on the 22d and the command was temporarily assigned to our commander, Col. Clark. As Lieut. Col. Shumway was left on the boat, Major Southmayd took command of the two battalions on shore. We marched some five miles toward Santiago, across country, the march being along a narrow and rough trail and halted for the night by the side of the trail. On our way we had to ford a stream and began to experience some of the realities of war.

That night we had to face our first real experience at going hungry. It had been understood that we were not to go inland that day and that rations would be sent us from the ships so no orders to take any with us had been issued. A few of the men had the foresight to stuff whatever food they could into their haversacks but the majority had nothing and went supperless to bed. The regulars bivouacked near us were in the same fix and there was much grumbling. However, officers and men were in the same box and there was nothing to do but make the best of it.

At dawn the next morning we rolled up our outfits and started off again. Our method of packing up was expeditious. Each man carried one half of a shelter tent, better known to us as a "dog" tent and later "pup" tents because of their small size, they being just about large enough for two men to crawl into. The half shelter was laid on the ground and upon it was spread first the rubber blanket and then the woolen one. Our canvas blouses and whatever personal property we had were then placed on top, together with the tent sticks and pegs and the whole neatly rolled. The ends were secured with the tent rope and the roll thus formed was carried over the left shoulder, the ends hanging down on the right side of the body. Thus equipped, with our full canteens and empty haversacks, we took to the road again after our first night on Cuban soil. Details of men from each company were sent back to the ships after rations and we started for Siboney. An early morning march on an empty stomach is not conducive to an appreciation of scenery be it ever so grand, but some of us enjoyed it. All about us were hills and mountains, their peaks clear cut against the blue sky, while from the tops of two or three rose thin smoke columns which we supposed were from signal fires. Our trail led us through valleys and over hills until finally about 11 o'clock we struck upon something that looked like a road and on which we were enabled to march for a short time in columns of fours. Anyone who had ever seen the Second on a parade in Springfield or Worcester or at camp and seen us straggling along the Cuban trail in single file would have laughed outright at the contrast, as we were forced to ourselves. Later on we looked even worse.

That day the "stripping" process, familiar to all armies in a campaign, was begun. Two companies of the second battalion, E and M had "toted" their knapsacks with them from their transports and about the second day out they were sorry for so doing. Hardly had we been an hour on the march that morning before the knapsacks began to disappear and the troops which followed us soon knew that the Second Massachusetts had passed by, meeting scores of Cubans with E and M company knapsacks on their backs and sweltering but happy in the closely buttoned cape overcoats discarded with the knapsacks. Fortunately our knapsacks and all our heavy baggage had been left on board ship but it was not long before we found our rolls becoming heavy and burdensome. Pretty soon a man would quietly drop out of the line, off would come his roll which was quickly opened, and some article he fancied he could do without, thrown into the bush. Then the roll would be fastened together, thrown over the owner's shoulder and he would hasten to rejoin his company. A few moments afterward a ragged Cubano might be seen poking around about the bushes and next the discarded articles would be in his possession.

And it may as well be told here that it was not only the Second Massachusetts that strewed more or less valuable or necessary articles along the trails. The regulars were with us in that, and although, as a rule, they had brought less baggage ashore with them than we did, they soon found it convenient to get rid of much of it. They even discarded their blankets, some cutting them in half and retaining only one part, while we stuck to the blankets and sacrificed other things. We never were sorry either that we kept our blankets, for if the days were intensely warm, the nights were cool and coverings came in handy.

That afternoon, soon after we had struck the short piece of good road referred to above, we left it and following a narrow trail debouched into some woods and after passing through them, found ourselves in a cocoanut grove. There were hundreds of the trees all laden with the fruit, and a halt was ordered, arms stacked and we were allowed to rest. About this time we were decidedly hungry, our breakfast having consisted of nothing and our dinner menu being the same. The cocoanuts looked inviting but they were far away at the tops of the branchless trees. But hunger is a spur and it was not long before some daring ones were "shinning up" the trees and down came the fruit. Alas! It was a disappointment to hopes of a satisfactory meal. After the hard, green outer husks had been chopped away it was found that the cocoanuts were green, and a copious flow of soldier language greeted this discovery. But it was not long before it was discovered that the milk of the green cocoanut makes a very palatable drink, and in a few moments we all became milkmen.

The march resumed we struck into another piece of woods, forded a brook or two, (we had by this time gotten over minding our feet being wet,) and found ourselves once more on a narrow and rough trail. On our way through the woods we saw stretched along a rough fence, the body of a huge snake of the constrictor variety, not long killed and looking decidedly fierce. The reptile was about eight feet long and as thick as a man's arm. A little further along we saw something which indicated that we were in a rough country. This was a human skull nailed on top of a post and grinning at us with empty eye sockets and toothless jaws, as we passed.

A little further along and we struck another narrow stream which, of course, had to be forded, and up a hill, just beyond that we came to a railroad station and the track. Here were some of our advance guard, men of the Eighth regulars who informed us that Siboney was "just 'round the corner," as one of them put it, and sure enough after a few moments more of the "Weary Willie" act, we came to a collection of "shacks," and realized that we were in Siboney. Now that word "Siboney" means much to us because it reminds us that there we ate, a fact sufficiently momentous on that day to linger long in our memories.

Now as to the methods of our eating. It was only a short time before our arrival that the Spaniards had evacuated Siboney after firing a few shots at our advance guard and the natives, who had "jumped the town" when the Spaniards told them there was going to be a big battle in which they were going to annihilate the "pigs of Yanquis," were just beginning to come back. We were ordered to camp on a low piece of ground on one side of the railroad embankment and after putting up our "pup" tents a few hungry ones went into the town to see what could be seen and incidentally to acquire what there was to acquire in the commissary line. They were successful in the latter. The natives were glad to see them and freely gave of what little they had. This wasn't much but there was some rice and some queer looking but good tasting messes of which our men were freely invited to partake. In one house in particular there were two aged women who busied themselves for hours cooking rice and other dishes for our men and who at first would not accept anything in payment. Finally it was forced upon them and before evening there was more silver money in that poor "shack" than had probably been the case for many a day.

All through the village it was the same and the hospitality we received at Siboney did much to change for a time the unfavorable opinion we had formed of the Cubans.

Not only was there food but drink. There was cool water in all the houses and there was also "bino," a sour Cuban wine like claret and some fiery "rou" or rum which brought tears to the eyes of more than one man who thought he was spirit proof. All that afternoon we mingled freely with the people, looked all through the town, examined with interest the Spanish block houses and some of us went in surf bathing on the pretty little beach in front of the town.

Late that afternoon the third battalion came up and about the same time the details which had been sent back for rations, made their appearance with about enough provisions to whet our appetite, they having found the task of lugging supplies for a company, nearly ten miles, beyond their strength.

CHAPTER X.

IN WHICH IS TO BE FOUND THE TALE OF "CRAB HOLLOW" AND SOME OTHER THINGS.

WHEN we retired to our luxurious couches that night of June 23d, most of us, excepting the guards, anticipated sleep, but we little recked what that night had in store for us. As told before, our camp was pitched on a low piece of ground and among a lot of sparse bushes. We did not know until the next day that the camping ground was an old burial place, and we were also not well enough up in the natural history of things Cuban to understand that if there is any one place the dainty land crab prefers for its habitat it is a cemetery and this preference rests upon a purely gastronomic basis. The land crab and the vulture are the great scavengers of Cuba and while the latter disposes of anything eatable left above ground the land crab looks after bodies or anything else placed under ground. In the afternoon we had noticed the holes of the land crabs but paid little attention to them, and only saw a few of the crustaceans, but at night we made their acquaintance at close quarters. We were pretty well fagged out with the heat and the marching, and this, with the strange sensation of having something to eat in our stomachs, tended to drowsiness. But hardly had we got settled in our tents before there were strange rustlings and noises and then the sensation of something crawling. There were some quick arisings and the sound of matches hastily struck and then exclamations and profanity. In some of the companies there was hardly a tent that had not been pitched over one or more land crab holes and the occupants of these had begun an investigation. Crawling over the sleepers usually resulted in awakening them and then came the exclamations, the illumination by the matches and the pursuit and slaughter of the visitors. The land crab is not an aggressive animal towards man and the greeting tendered him usually resulted in his scuttling for his hole. Not always did he reach there, for many fell victims to ramrods, clubs and other weapons. One able bodied crab was caught in the act of backing into his hole with a stocking in his claws, and yielded up his life for his rapacity. It may have been that he intended to eat the stocking, and had he done so his fate would have been the same anyway. The crabs had a pleasant trick that night of crawling half way up the outside of the tents and then losing their hold and dropping to the ground. That was bad enough as a deterrent to sleep, but it was not all. In the afternoon some I company men had repaired a locomotive disabled by the Spaniards, and kept running it up and down the tracks, to an accompaniment of bell and whistle, until a late hour.

Bright and early the next morning we were up and as on the day before looking for grub. Rations were still "shy" and once more we had recourse to our friends the Siboneyians who gave us what they could, which was not much, as their own supplies were running low.

Meanwhile the remainder of the transports had come to Siboney and were landing the rest of the expedition. They had a little different method of doing it than at Daiquiri. The boats would be filled with men and towed in as near shore as possible when the men would have to jump out and wade ashore. Some of them didn't like getting their feet wet but they had to just the same.

It was some little time before noon when we heard firing from over the hills and learned that the cavalry brigade had gone on a reconnoisance in force in that direction. It was only a short time afterwards when we saw the first wounded begin to come down the trail and learned that they had found the enemy in force at Las Guasimas and had quite a go with him. The First and Tenth United States cavalry, our old neighbors at Lakeland, and the Rough Riders were engaged and from all accounts were having a warm time. Col. Clark of the Second was acting as commander of our brigade and receiving orders from Gen. Lawton to reinforce the cavalry, left for the scene with the Eighth and Twenty-second Infantry. They arrived there just as the Spaniards were running and finding nothing for them to do returned to Siboney.

One of the largest buildings in the town had been converted into a temporary hospital and it was soon filled with the wounded. Our regimental surgeons, Drs. Bowen, Gates and Hitchcock were pressed into service and rendered valuable aid. That hospital was our first introduction to some of the grim realities of war but the boys stood it well and were anxious to get to the front as quickly as possible. One of the warships with the transports added to the excitement by shelling the woods on top of a point near us and we began to conclude it would be our turn next.

But it was not long before our thoughts were turned from the vision of great deeds in battle to a more prosaic but necessary matter. A lot of rations had been landed and soon we were revelling in such delicacies as hardtack, "sowbelly" bacon, coffee, canned beef (?) and canned tomatoes. Orders were issued for each man to take four days' rations but our haversack capacity was not equal to this and we packed all we could into our rolls. Even then we could not take all the issue and what was left we gave to our friends, the people of Siboney, who gladly accepted what we didn't want. The issue was hardly begun before Col. Clark gave us orders to move and off we started about 4.30 in the afternoon. We had not gone far in the direction of Las Guasimas before we came to the conclusion that the commissary department of the army had at least one genius who deserved a medal and some other things. About half the issue of tomatoes was in gallon cans and it was planned to have one man carry them a short distance and then let another sharer of the can relieve him. But our route lay up hill and we hit up a lively pace so that it was not long before there was a "kick" about the tomatoes. The ending of the kick in every case was a noise which indicated that the can had landed in the bushes and when tired out, we reached our bivouac place that night there were but few gallon cans of tomatoes left with the outfit.

Meanwhile we kept steadily climbing up into the hills, finding rough footing and stumbling over rocks and everything else in the darkness until about 9 o'olock we reached the scene of the battle and found the First and Tenth cavalry burying their dead. We passed on in silence but we did quite a bit of thinking. A short distance further up we halted on a level bit of ground by the side of the Rough Riders and after making our simple preparations for our night's bivouac heard their tale of the fight. Our cooking fires were soon going and we not only heard Roosevelt's men tell their experiences and gave them our sympathy, but what they wanted more at that particular time, we gave them food, sharing our rations with them. One New York paper, in its story of the Las Guasimas fight spoke of the Second Massachusetts as having "supported the Rough Riders," but so far as we knew our only support to them was that night when we certainly did support them with our rations.

When we landed in Cuba a detail of men from each company was left on the boats to look after property and as we learned afterwards they heard all sorts of stories about what happened to us that day. But all the stories agreed that the

Second had been having a bad time of it and that our loss was heavy. One New York newspaper man had been given a circumstantial account of our regiment having been surrounded by the Spaniards and of our cutting our way out with a heavy loss in officers and men and was so impressed by it that he wrote a very pretty story which he was on the point of having cabled to his paper when a brother correspondent happened along and convinced him that as we were at Siboney until the action was all over we could hardly have been so badly cut up. So the story was not cabled but it was a narrow escape.

When we left Siboney that afternoon G company was left behind to assist in unloading supplies for our brigade, one company from each regiment being detailed for that purpose. They left Siboney early the next morning and reached us just as we were preparing to resume the march again.

Our next camping place was on a plateau near where had once been a sizeable plantation and which was only a short distance from Las Guasimas. Here we remained two days taking life easy before we again took up the march. On the 27th we reached Sevilla and there remained until late in the the afternoon of June 30th. During our stay in Sevilla occurred another food shortage and also the great tobacco famine. Rations were hard to get and so were medicines. There was so much feeling over the delinquency in getting our supplies up to us that a meeting of the company commanders was held and a committee appointed to wait upon Col. Clark to see if something could not be done. The outcome of all the talk was the loan of some of the horses of the field and staff to a detail which, in charge of Lieut. Vesper of B, went back to the ships and obtained a small supply of provisions and tobacco. The cause of the failure to keep the troops supplied lay with the quartermaster's department which had apparently broken down utterly, for though there were tons upon tons of supplies already landed at Siboney there was not enough of pack trains or other means of transportation to get them up to us. We all fared alike at this time, officers and men, regulars and volunteers, and our brigade, the leading one in the army, had been hustled along so fast that it was difficult under any circumstances to get supplies to us owing to the distance and the condition of the roads.

On the 28th the new commander of the brigade, Gen. Ludlow, reported and relieved Col. Clark who resumed command of the Second. Lieut. Harry Parkhurst of K who had been acting as aide-de-camp on the brigade staff was also relieved and rejoined his company.

The tobacco famine was relieved somewhat by some of the weed brought from the ships by the various "relief expeditions" and also by the arrival of the details which had been left on the boats and the majority of the members of which had gained permission to rejoin us as soon as they heard the stories about our having been in action and losing heavily. The horse detail also came up and brought to Adjutant Hawkins the news that his horse had been drowned while being got ashore. As the chaplain's horse and one owned by Hospital Steward Fortier had been stolen while in Tampa by "Billy the Hostler" there was a shyness of horses around headquarters.

While in Tampa Private T. C. Boone of K had been transferred to the signal corps with the rank of sergeant and afterwards became a member of the war balloon squad. On the afternoon of the 20th we saw the famous balloon for the first time and watched it with interest as it rose above the trees near our camp. We understood that Boone was one of the men in the car and for that reason the balloon had more than usual interest for us of the Springfield companies. The next afternoon another ascension was made and again we watched the "big gas bag" and speculated in a pessimistic vein upon its successful use. Our doubts as to its usefulness turned out to be correct.

On the 28th the good news was announced that we could send mail home that afternoon and there was great scrambling for pens, pencils, paper and envelopes. It was our first opportunity since we had landed to send letters and that it was taken advantage of the big mail bags that left headquarters late that afternoon for division headquarters attested.

Probably the condition in which about all our letters reached the folks at home was fully explained soon after our return, but it will bear retelling. When we landed most of us had paper, envelopes and stamps. But these were carried either in the haversacks or rolls and with the heat the envelope flaps became stuck together, likewise the stamps and paper became dirty. All were about in the same condition, so in order to get a letter into an envelope it was necessary to slit the latter at one end, insert the letter and then sew up the envelope. As most of the sewing was done with black thread and the envelopes were not especially clean the effect upon the good folks at home must have been rather startling, especially when the letters came without stamps, as they usually did. In place of stamps the government allowed the use of the words, "Soldier's Letter" in one corner of the envelope and when indorsed by an officer was allowed to go through.

From our camp we could see a portion of the fortifications of Santiago and especially two large buildings which we were informed were barracks that had been transformed into hospitals and over which we could with field glasses see a number of Red Cross flags floating. We heard many weird tales as to what the Spaniards had done and would do and the stories, mainly of Cubans, as to how many troops were in the city, varied all the way from 10,000 to 40,000. On the 29th the much talked of "army" of Gen. Calixto Garcia arrived and it was a motley looking outfit, mostly black in color and of great variety, principally of lack of quantity, as to uniforms but fairly well supplied with arms and ammunition. The knowledge of English of the component parts of Garcia's forces was about equal to our knowledge of Spanish, but considerable interchange of ideas was effected, principally by signs. One or two of the warriors would stroll into camp and after standing around a bit with the inevitable Cuban grin would exclaim, "*Santiago, boum, boum?*" at the same time pointing to the city. We could do no less than to assure them there would be plenty of "*boum, boum*" and that when it happened Santiago would be "on the bum." The ice thus broken, the Cuban's machete was examined and the wearer induced to give an exhibition of its use both as a weapon and a handy tool for many purposes. Generally before they left camp they would "borrow" some "tobac" and if they could obtain some hardtack or bacon they went away happy. Sometimes they brought us some mangoes or "monkey plums" and then would follow some great bartering. The surgeons in an excess of zeal had warned us against the mango but we pinned our faith to the Cubans' declaration that if one didn't eat mangoes and drink liquor on the same day no evil effects would result from the free and unlimited use of the fruit. The mango tastes nice but it is an acquired art to know how to eat it without getting three-quarters of it over one's face and clothing. Still it came in handy when our rations were short, which was about always and we were not over fastidious as to how we ate anything in those days.

CHAPTER XI.

WHICH TELLS HOW WE GOT READY TO TAKE THE TOWN OF EL CANEY.

IT was shortly after noon on June 30th that the "JoJo" department began to circulate the news that we were to move on to Santiago that day or the next and for the first and only time during the campaign the "JoJo" happened to be right. Orders had arrived for a forward movement and although we had no idea of where we were to go or what we were to do there was a feeling of satisfaction that we were to go somewhere and do something.

Of even more importance than the orders at this particular time was the arrival of a well laden pack train with rations. When the mules were first discerned coming "up the pike" it was supposed they were carrying ammunition as the last two or three pack trains had brought little excepting cartridges. But this time we were agreeably disappointed. There was a plentiful supply of "sowbelly," hardtack and coffee and it was not long before it was being distributed. The tobacco famine had temporarily been relieved and now we actually had food. So we were pretty well satisfied with life after all.

How it rained that day! It came on in the forenoon and in less than ten minutes everybody and everything was saturated. It was a straight downpour of water and rubber blankets were of little use in keeping us or our belongings dry so we simply got wet and stayed in that condition until the sun came out and did his best to dry things up quickly.

Early that afternoon we saw the war balloon again and watched it with much interest, everybody "rubbernecking" at the unwonted sight. In the car, although we did not know it at the time, was poor "Tom" Boone of "K" and those of us who knew him little recked what the next day would bring to him. For that matter there was considerable uncertainty as to what the future meant for any of us. We heard late in the day that we were sure to get into action on the next day but somehow the knowledge did not appear to worry but a few of the boys. The happenings of the campaign thus far had done much to produce a feeling of contempt for the fighting abilities of the Spaniards and some of us figured that all we would have to do was to make a demonstration in force and the enemy would then either retreat or surrender. How mistaken we were the next day was to tell us.

It was late in the afternoon when the advance on El Caney by Lawton's division was begun and it was not until almost 6 o'clock that our brigade, which being one of the nearest to the city, was among the last to get away, made its start. Most of us will never forget that night march. The rain of the morning had resulted as usual in making whatever roads and trails there were into very fine specimens of mud puddles and unfortunately for us the greater part of our way led up hill. When the rations were issued in the afternoon the company commissaries had not time to complete their distribution and thinking that the march was to be a short and easy one those of G and B concluded that it would be better to have some of the provisions carried in bulk rather than to take time to divide and issue them. So a number of men from each company were detailed to carry a couple of slabs of "sowbelly" and others the remaining boxes of hardtack. This worked very nicely for a time until it became dark and the hill climbing act began. Then there was trouble. The trail up the hill was about as slippery as any we ever marched along in Cuba and it was moreover filled with rocks and boulders over which climbing was not the easiest matter in the world. Before they had gone very far the ration detail began to think that something was wrong and these thoughts developed into a certainty as we still kept climbing along up a pretty steep ascent and the boxes of hardtack and the sides of bacon (?) began to grow heavier and heavier and more difficult to handle. For convenience in packing them along with us both Sergeants Scully and Bearse had nailed long handles onto the hardtack boxes and had made a somewhat similar arrangement to carry the bacon but the carriers had not gone far before the handles worked off and after awhile it got to be a question of dropping the rations or killing the men trying to carry them. It was pitch dark, the trail was difficult and besides all the men had a pretty fair supply of "grub" in their haversacks, so a silent and informal vote was taken and the bulk of the extra rations were quietly left by the side of the trail. Meanwhile the rest of us were not having so much of a picnic even though we were not encumbered with extra baggage. The mud made marching difficult even along the road which led from the camp. Soon we left this and came to the San Juan creek, passing a company of soldiers who were actually bathing. Our surprise at this unwonted scene was not allowed to last long, for the trail lay on the other side of the creek and we were obliged to ford it. This was not by any means as easy as it looked. The banks were high and slippery with mud and the water was over our legging tops but in we plunged and scrambled across to the other side and into a thick piece of woods, shaking the water from ourselves dog fashion as we again took up the march. Hardly had we got across before low spoken orders came down the line for every man to keep silent and to march as quietly as possible. This made us realize that something was on and the orders were pretty well obeyed although all the orders in the world could not keep some of the men from saying things concerning the trail and night marches in general.

In ragged fashion we stumbled along through the woods, the only military regulation we followed out being that of keeping well "closed up." We simply had to do this because it was so dark and the trail so narrow and rough that unless one kept very "close tabs" on his file leader it was a question of getting lost and going it alone and this none of us desired to do.

We had not gone far before we came to another creek or it may have been another turn of the first one, we did not know or care which, but into it we plunged and again got our feet wet and muddy. Hardly had we gained the other side before we came across a forlorn looking figure in a bit of a clearing by the side of the trail and a voice with an unmistakeable western twang inquired if we were the Rough Riders. The owner of the voice was informed that we were the Second Massachusetts and he then remarked, "Well, you're a pretty good outfit and I guess I'll go along with you." He then announced himself as the chaplain of the Rough Riders and said he had left camp a little behind his regiment and had not only been unable to catch up with it but could obtain no trace of its whereabouts. We told him his regiment had probably gone over towards San Juan hill, it being in another division than ours and he then allowed that he would not bother looking further that night but would accompany us. We made no objection and he trudged along with us for the rest of the way.

Soon after meeting the chaplain we forded creek number three but by this time we were used to getting our feet wet and did not mind it much. After fording this stream, a narrow but rather deep one, we began to get up in the world and soon discovered that we were on the up grade. For nearly two hours more we stumbled along, sometimes passing through thick woods and again along open country. The moon came out faintly after a bit, but her light did little towards revealing to us the difficulties of the route we were following. We had a couple of brief halts but it was not until a little after 10 o'clock that a whispered command to halt was given and we were informed that we were to go into bivouac by the road side.

Following this order came a renewal of the previous ones against making any noise and we were also given strict orders not to make a fire or even strike a match. These precautions we assumed were to keep our presence unknown to the enemy and although most of us wanted the comfort of a pipe or cigarette after our fatiguing march yet we refrained. There was of course much speculation over the why and wherefore of the night march and the orders against noise or fire but the generally accepted assumption was that we had stolen a march upon the Spaniards, had penetrated their lines, and in the morning would march into Santiago before the astonished enemy had partaken of his morning coffee. This surmise was given color by the fact that from where we were we could look down into the city, its locality being indicated by the lights from the governor general's palace and other official buildings. We were on a plateau that overlooked the city, and so far as we could judge, our presence was absolutely undetected. Santiago appeared to be sleeping peacefully and looked for all the world like some small New England city which is locked up every night at 8.30 or 9 and whose residents then go to bed and stay there until morning.

For thinking such thoughts we were indeed what are known in the vernacular as "good things," for as it transpired afterwards the Spaniards knew all about where we were and where we were going. Had it not been for their traditional

Lehigh Detail from Company H

policy of "manana" they might have sallied out and done several things to us, but they preferred to wait until the next day, which was a lucky thing for us.

Sleep comes quickly to a soldier in bivouac and soon after our halt every one of us, with the exception of the guards, was asleep. No attempt was made to put up the shelter tents, but we contented ourselves with unrolling them, spreading them upon the grass and wrapping ourselves up in our blankets. A few of us lunched upon hardtack and raw bacon washed down with muddy water from the canteens but the majority of the boys were too tired to think even of eating.

That night the premonition came to some of our boys that the morrow would be their last day on earth and although we tried to laugh it out of them they stuck to it that their fate was settled. One of these boys was Frank Moody of K and so strongly was he impressed with the feeling of coming disaster to himself that he made one of his comrades take his watch and promise to deliver his farewell message to the loved ones at home.

Tired soldiers sleep soundly and it seemed as if we had only slumbered a few moments when we were awakened, not by the usual bugle call, but by low whispers from the officers and non-commissioned officers. It was hardly dawn and a thin mist concealed from view the city below us and the hills that surrounded us. Little by little the mist disappeared before the advance of the sun and when dawn came the scene was so impressive in its grandeur that even the most careless amongst us felt it. Just below us was Santiago still wrapped in the morning mist and apparently still unaroused from its slumbers. All about us were frowning hills and mountains and in the distance we could see the harbor outside of which sat the grim war ships of the United States waiting for their prey to come out and be eaten up. Not a sign from the enemy and we wondered.

But we wondered even more when we turned our eyes a little to the right and there saw Capron's light battery, still unlimbered and apparently in plain view of the sentries of the enemy and our wonder increased as we saw the smoke from the cooking fires of the batterymen and watched them preparing their morning meal. For, be it understood, our brigade commander had sent word along that the orders of the night before as to noise and fires were still in force and we had breakfasted on hardtack and water. And there were the artillerymen with their fires lighted and frying their bacon and making their coffee as if there were no such orders and not a Spaniard within fifty miles. We could not understand it and for that matter we do not to this day. Maybe somebody does but if so we never heard of it.

It was bad enough to almost smell the hot coffee, for the morning air was cool and raw, and to see the batterymen drinking it with relish, but it was far worse to see them nonchalantly light their pipes and cigarettes and enjoy them. Since the night before we had been deprived of the solace of tobacco and anyone who has ever soldiered knows what that means. But when we saw the red striped gunners enjoying the weed we made up our minds to follow suit. In a very short time our pipes were going and the officers sympathetically not only forebore to stop us but soon began to puff their pipes. Even a cold breakfast can be enjoyed with a tobacco dessert and that early morning smoke on the threshold of the battlefield was a much appreciated one.

Meanwhile we had been getting ready and as packing up did not take us long it was but a short time after we were aroused from our slumbers before we had fallen in and were ready for what the day might bring forth. While waiting for orders to march we heard the noise of hoofs coming up the trail and Gen. Lawton and his staff clattered by us on their way to the front. A couple of Cuban officers were with them and they were evidently pleased with the work cut out for the Americans that day. Only a few moments after the general had passed came the orders to march and we were soon "hitting the trail" again, this time on the down grade.

It was then about 4.30 in the morning. We moved along slowly, the trail being so narrow it was necessary to go in column of files and it was fully as bad walking as the route we had gone over the previous night. After a little we came to a brook and took advantage of the opportunity to fill our canteens. Just on the other side of the brook we passed Capron's battery posted on a low hill, the muzzles of the three inch rifles pointed toward El Caney and the cannoneers at their posts waiting for the ball to open. By that time we all realized that this was the day we were to go into business.

CHAPTER XII.

WHEREIN IS RELATED SOME EVENTS WHICH HAPPENED TO US ON JULY FIRST.

HARDLY had we passed the battery before we heard the boom of one of its guns, followed by another and another and we knew then the trouble had begun. We kept on the trail for a while longer, the men keeping well closed up now and keeping eyes and ears alert. El Caney was now replying to Capron and we could hear for the first time the squeal of the Mauser bullets as they began to go over us with a sound like that of a vicious cat at bay. We were under fire but hardly realized it as yet.

It was a splendid morning. Our trail led along the side of what had once been well cultivated fields, the only indication of that now being the inevitable barbed wire fencing. The skies were cloudless and birds sang as we went along to battle. There were other birds too but they did not sing. Hardly had the first of Capron's cannon sent its "good morning" salute to El Caney before a speck was visible in the sky. Larger and larger it grew until we saw it was a buzzard scenting the battle and before long it was joined by hundreds of its kind, all circling about in the air only a short distance from the earth and waiting for the rich feast about to be spread for them. But we recked not of buzzards or what their presence presaged.

A short distance further along the trail, a quick order and we changed direction to the right, leaving the trail and going across the field directly toward El Caney. Barbed wire fencing was in our way but the two wire cutters attached to each company soon made a gate for us. Our battalion swung through and into the field while the second battalion kept to the trail and took the field further along. The third battalion and I of the second, as we afterwards found, were halted by Capron's battery and were not given front seats to the performance. The field soon changed to scrub and bush through which way was made as best we could without much regard to alignment. Then came a bit of forest and then we debouched out upon the Santiago road, one of the few thoroughfares in Cuba that looked like a road. A halt and then we stripped for action. Rolls and haversacks were taken off and piled by the road side. The belts and the pockets of the brown canvas coats were filled with cartridges and we were ready for trouble.

Meanwhile it was evident that there was trouble ahead of the Second. From El Caney's forts and trenches came a hail of bullets, while on our right and left there were the Krags of our regulars popping away with machine like regularity, their whip like sentences being punctuated at intervals by the 3-inch rifles of Capron's men. Over our heads went the Mausers in a steady stream and there wasn't a man of the Second marching up that road that morning who failed to bow his head, (most of us called it "ducking") in response to their salutation. The 8th and 22d of our brigade had gone on ahead of us, had deployed to the left and we could hear their Krags answering the Mausers. It was our first experience under fire and it is no wonder that nearly all of us wished ourselves, for just a few moments, somewhere else and remembered certain pressing engagements we had at Springfield that Friday morning. But this feeling was like going into a cold bath. The first plunge is the worst and within half an hour after getting into the action these same men that were "ducking" their heads to the bullets were up on the firing line and acting like veterans instead of men who up to that morning had never faced an armed foe. Our education had progressed rapidly.

And here a word as to El Caney where Gen. Vara Del Ray and 620 Spanish troops held Lawton's division at bay from 6.30 in the morning until 4.30 in the afternoon. In the general plan for the day's work of July 1st Lawton's division was to sweep over to Caney, devote an hour or so to capturing it and then swing over to the San Juan forts and aid Kent's division to take them. Trustworthy (?) Cuban advices were that there were only a couple of hundred Spanish troops in El Caney and the taking of that outpost of Santiago was to be but an incident of our march to San Juan. But Gen. Del Ray had not been consulted as to this program and the result was our time schedule went to pieces. An entire division against 620 men looks like heavy odds in favor of the division but it must be remembered that the enemy were strongly entrenched with all the advantage of position and knew the ground thoroughly, while we were in the open with little or no shelter and with only a four-gun light battery against stone forts, strong blockhouses and well made intrenchments, so that our advavtage in numbers was more than made up by the superior position of the enemy.

El Caney lay almost directly in front of us, a small town backed up against a steep hill as if at bay and with forts, intrenchments and houses bristling with rifles. To our right on a small elevation was the famous stone fort over which floated the red and yellow flag of Spain. A little to the left was the village church, of stone and converted into a fortress while on either sides of both fort and church were the familiar Spanish blockhouses. And in front of all were the trenches, well built and covering all the front and sides of the town, a covered way connecting some of them with the fort and with their fronts guarded by fences and entanglements of barbed wire, a protection found of value against the Cubans, but which proved to be of less efficiency against the valor of American soldiers. This was what El Caney presented to us on that bright July morning.

Our brigade's work had been mapped out and appeared to be comparatively easy. It was to take position' on the left of the American line and cut off the retreat of the enemy towards Santiago when he was driven from Caney which, as already scheduled, was to be within an hour or so after the initial shot. But the program for Ludlow‚s brigade was changed by force of circumstances, for hardly had the 8th and 22d of our brigade got into position before they were attacked and replied in kind and within a few moments the hottest part of the action was taking place on the left instead of being confined to the right and center, as originally planned.

And while this was happening we were down the "pike" getting ready to add our contribution to the din of battle. We were not long in getting ready and leaving one man from each company to guard the rolls left by the roadside the seven companies of the Second marched to the firing line. The first battalion, G, B, K and D companies, was by this time some distance ahead of the second, while the third was still held up by the battery. Col. Clark, Lieut. Col. Shumway and Adjutant Hawkins were standing beneath a huge tree at the intersection of the "sunken" road with the Santiago road and hardly had the companies come up before an order came from Gen. Ludlow to send four companies to strengthen the line of the 22d on our left. B and K companies of the first battalion and L and E of the second battalion, which had by this time come up, were detailed and B and K, under command of Major Southmayd started for the 22d. L and E followed but through some misunderstanding got into a "hot box" and after a time returned to the sunken road and took position there.

B and K marched down the sunken road and then across an open space, across which the bullets were flying in a steady stream. It was necessary to "duck" here and it was done without any loss of dignity. This space cleared, the companies came to a bit of bush and then into a gully facing El Caney on the left. Here was the 22d, lying down and answering the fire of the Spaniards in good style.

Hardly had B and K reached the gully and taken position when the hail of bullets began to fall among them and men began to drop. Private Frank E. Moody of K was one of the first hit and died almost instantly, the bullet having pierced his heart. On the march of the night before he had felt a presentiment of his fate and so strong was this feeling of his fate that he gave his watch to Private Fuller to take home to his parents. Before long Private John J. Malone of B got a fatal wound just below the heart and then men began to fall thick and fast. As soon as the two companies had taken their positions they were ordered to fire, but the enemy's return for the first few volleys was payment with compound interest. The smoke from the Springfield rifles showed the position of our men and lifting slowly, made just the target which the enemy needed. At this time the line was about 900 yards from the advanced Spanish trenches and it must have been just like rifle practice for the enemy. Within a moment after the first volley from the Springfields crashed out a hail of bullets was poured into the two companies from the trenches and men fell like sheep. Capt. Warriner, raising on one shoulder to give an order, sank back with a Mauser through his body. Corporal Ward Lathrop got one through his head, Corporal Hoadley got his "in the neck," the bullet going through the right side, Wagoner Boulè had one through his left hand, Private Ashley of B was hit in the left forearm, Private James F. Ferrier was shot through the right shoulder and also had a

bullet traverse the right side of his head, making an ugly wound, Howard Meyrick had a double one, one bullet striking his right leg, while another went through his left shoulder and the upper part of his left arm. Private C. J. Riordan got a bullet through his left hand while Private A. E. Rose got the thumb and one finger of his right hand nipped. Private W. B. Riopel was hard hit, the bullet entering his left shoulder and entering the lungs. Backman of K got a Mauser through his left elbow and was also hit in the left leg below the knee.

As quickly as possible the wounded were picked up by their comrades and taken to the rear, a temporary dressing station being established beneath a huge tree on the Santiago road. The first aid bandages came in handily on the field and were used to advantage. Lieut. Powers took command of K and Capt. McDonald, as cool as if battles were everyday occurrences, kept a watchful eye on his men.

The heavy fire which the powder smoke had drawn upon the two companies was also being felt by the 22d and its choleric commander, Major Van Horn, came rushing over with, "For God's sake, Second Massachusetts, stop firing! You're making us a regular target for the enemy." This was not all he said, either, but it was stronger language than politeness required. The firing did stop, that is, the volley firing did, but the company commanders gave their men orders to fire at will. Soon Major Van Horn came over with another protest and the two companies moved along a little further to the right but on the same line as the 22d and leaving quite a little gap between them. As the 22d advanced so did B and K, taking advantage of what cover there was and keeping up their fire for some time. It was perhaps that protest of Major Van Horn that gave the impression that the entire Second regiment was ordered off the firing line, an impression that is a very much mistaken one. From the time the two companies took position on the right of the 22d they fired at intervals and at will until the Spaniards were driven from the last trench and El Caney was taken.

While these things were happening on our left G company was having troubles of its own on the extreme right of the line. Sending B and K to the 22d left Col. Clark with only G and D companies of the first battalion with him, the three companies of the second battalion having been placed in the sunken road, whose banks gave them some protection from the incessant fire from El Caney. G and D were sent further along up the Santiago road and G was halted directly in front of a cultivated field which was directly in front of the trenches and the town and was flanked by the stone fort. Halting here the second platoon of the company under Lieut. Edward J. Leyden deployed as skirmishers and advanced across the field, taking every possible advantage of cover, of which there was little, and halting at intervals to kneel and fire. The light brown uniforms advancing slowly across the field soon attracted the notice of the enemy, even before the first volley from the Springfields gave the Spaniards a target, and men began to drop. Still the line advanced until it was within 500 yards of the fort and then a halt was ordered and the men threw themselves flat on the ground and began firing at will. Now the bullets from both fort and trenches were hailing about them but they kept crawling along until within a range of 400 yards. Then Lieut. Leyden looked around and saw that his 14 men were isolated from the rest of the company and he at once realized that it was suicidal to go further without reinforcements. Arthur Packard, beloved of all his comrades, had fallen dead on the field with a Spanish bullet through his head and George Richmond, one of the "old timers" of the company, had fallen fatally wounded. "Goldie" Bresnan had been ordered to the rear with the blood dripping from a shattered hand and Ernest Marble, wounded in the head, lay on the field. Others had in the meantime joined the little force, men from other companies,

but not enough to make a further advance successful.
Among the reinforcements was Lieut. D. J. Moynihan of I
company, who had left his position with the second battalion
and walked across the field to join Leyden's men. He
essayed his luck as a sharpshooter, borrowing a rifle from
one of the men, and fired three shots before he himself sank
to the ground with a bullet through his body. Before this
happened, however, and when he first joined Lieut. Leyden,
Lieut. Moynihan advised that the advance should continue
and suggested a charge. But Lieut. Leyden pointed to the
few men he had and asked what the result would be. There
was no answer to this. Less than 20 men charging against
a stone fort under a heavy fire from it and flanked by the
trenches would have been heroic, no doubt, but it would have
been deliberately throwing away men's lives and to no good
result. So Lieut. Leyden refused to order a charge but sent
Lieut. Moynihan back to Col. Clark for orders. These were
for him to remain where he was and there the platoon stayed
until the town was taken, although some of the men advanced even closer to the fort, taking advantage of some
small piles of stones, which had evidently been heaped up as
shelter for Spanish outposts. All the long afternoon the little
squad lay under the pitiless sun, firing whenever there was a
chance until they heard the cheers of the charging regulars
and saw the red and yellow flag of Spain go down from the
fort and the Stars and Stripes replace it. Then they sprang
to their feet and cheered. But it was not all over then.
The fort had been taken but from trench and blockhouse and
church and every building in El Caney still came the hail of
Mausers. The dead and wounded of the Second were being
attended to as best could be done, but their comrades still
fought on. Two guns of Capron's battery had been moved
up to a position in the rear of D company and the balance of
G and were knocking things about in the old town. Gen.
Vara Del Ray was wounded unto death and the American

troops were drawing their lines closer and closer around Caney, but still the Spaniards fought on with the courage of desperation. At the fork of the roads was Col. Clark, sending his staff officers, or rather officer, Lieut. Paul R. Hawkins, hither and thither and giving messages to his orderlies. Lieut. Hawkins, cool under fire, won a high place in the regard of the men who saw him that day and the orderlies, including Private Ross of B, showed coolness and courage. Two other Springfield men, Sergeant Scully and Corporal Ross of G were pressed into service as orderlies for a time and did their duty well. Two cool and collected men were Col. Clark and Lieut. Col. Shumway and both exposed themselves, at times against the wish of the brigade commander, along the line. Gen. Ludlow was for some time at the fork of the roads with Col. Clark, his dead horse, shot under him, almost at the outset of the action, lying near by, but once he was gone he did not return and neither he nor anyone else in authority gave the orders to withdraw the Second from the firing line, as has been stated by some. If any such orders were issued which is doubtful, they were never received by Col. Clark, and the companies of the Second stayed throughout the day where he placed them.

Meanwhile the big tree a bit down the road was the scene of some grewsome work. Soon after the opening of the action Lieut. Hawkins had been ordered by Col. Clark to bring up the surgeons and the ground under the big tree was then transformed into a temporary hospital or rather a dressing station. Here Surgeon Bowen and his assistants, Lieuts. Gates and Hitchcock, aided by Hospital Stewards Fortier, Greenberg and Howes and the members of the hospital corps, labored until the enemy's sharpshooters, discerning the group under the tree, made it an object of attention and the bullet-torn leaves began to flutter down upon the wounded. Then the hospital was moved farther down the road and the dead and dying and wounded conveyed there as tenderly as possible under the circumstances. It was here the heroic Father Edwin Fitzgerald, the beloved chaplain of the 22d, labored from morning until far into the night, caring as tenderly as a mother for the wounded of all the regiments, making their places as easy as possible for them, bringing them water from the distant brook, giving the consolations of religion to all, whether of his creed or not. More than once he visited the firing line and aided in bringing some poor fellow down to the hospital. Danger he cared not for and he went on with his work apparently oblivious to his bullet-torn coat, two holes in which bore eloquent witness to narrow escapes. On that day Father Fitzgerald earned the lifelong affection of the officers and men of the Second.

And so time wore on until between 4.30 and 5 in the afternoon, when ringing cheers announced that the last trench had been won and El Caney was ours. Then followed the reunion of the regiment. Lieut. Leyden marched his gallant platoon back and the men fell into their old places in G company. B and K came back from the left with the 22d and the regiment gathered once more on the Santiago road, soldiers now, stained with powder and battle smoke and grim with the thoughts of the day and its events. Further down the road in the improvised hospital lay the forms, cold in death, of five brave men and with them were 40 more or less seriously wounded, three of them mortally.

The Second had received its baptism of blood.

CHAPTER XIII.

WE LEARN SOME MORE THINGS ABOUT THE ART OF WAR AS CONDUCTED IN THESE DAYS.

IT was not exactly a joyous reunion as the companies assembled in the Santiago road that afternoon. True, we were all glad to see one another again, but the heat and burden of the day had been great and there were many faces missing from the ranks. Nearly ten hours on the battlefield under the burning Cuban sun and without much to comfort us in the way of food or drink was not conducive to good temper and to this was added the spur of the ingratitude of our so-called Cuban allies. It will be remembered that just before the regiment went into action the rolls and haversacks had been discarded and placed by the roadside and it fell out that while the owners were up on the firing line fighting for *Cuba Libre*, some of the Cuban patriots came along and, the guards placed over the property being absent, helped themselves to the rations in the haversacks. These were the Cubans, by the way, who were supposed to be fighting over on our left that day, but it seems they had more important business, to them, on hand to bother much about fighting. So as we gathered there in the road in the stillness which followed the battle storm and realized that we were to go supperless there were some things said about our Cuban friends which indicated a not very high feeling of esteem for them.

Once gathered together again and the roll called came the after work of the battle. Squads were sent over the field to bring in any dead or wounded that might have been overlooked and to gather up any property left there. The companies which had lost men prepared to march to the hospital to bury the dead and those fortunate ones whose haversacks had been untouched began to light their cooking fires. Hardly an hour had elapsed since Caney was taken when up came an aide with orders for Col. Clark and when he read them the assembly sounded and we heard with disgust the orders that the regiment was to move at once to San Juan to reinforce the first division. We had anticipated after our hard day's work a bite to eat and a night's rest and here we were disappointed in both. Faintly through that day at intervals we at Caney could hear the sounds of battle in our rear and we heard late in the afternoon that it was our troops attacking the San Juan forts but it was not until after we had finished our job at El Caney that we heard what the first division had done.

But orders are orders and grumbling does not count against them. The details sent to dig graves were recalled, the equipments were donned again and in a short time we were once more "piking the pike." It was a gloomy march that evening, for the men were not very much inclined to conversation. On we went, now in columns of fours on a fairly decent road for Cuba, again in column of files through the bush and finally emerged onto another road. It was now dark, but we kept on until about 10 o'clock we came to a stone bridge over the San Juan river and the order to halt was given as the head of our regiment reached the bridge. Whether it was to be a mere halt or a bivouac no one seemed to know and no one cared. Hardly had the order to halt been given before the men had dropped by the roadside and, worn out by the toilsome march of the night before and the day's work, followed by the march to the bridge, were asleep, many of them without even taking off their heavy rolls. It was not an ideal place for slumber, either. Troops were continually passing by and every now and then a mule team would pass with a clatter but the sleepers slumbered on. Until after midnight we lay there, waiting for further orders. About one o'clock up came mule wagons and a pack train and soon after the men were awakened and told to "hurry up" and get rations. In a few moments the scene was changed. Huge fires were lighted and by their light the rations were given out, the delights of slumber proving to be less strong than the desire to eat and every man awakening to the knowledge that we would soon be on the move again. So it was. Hardly had we drawn rations and began to cook them before a battery of artillery moved hurriedly by us to the rear, many of us just having time to draw our legs out of the way of the wheels. Next came the 8th and 22d of our brigade and by 2 o'clock we too were on the march. Following the road over which we had come for a short distance, we soon left it and changing direction to the right, swung into a trail across country. Along this we marched for hours amid the darkness, through woods and chaparral and fields, once cultivated. We climbed hills and forded streams, all in the darkness, we brushed the morning mist from the trees and grass as we passed, and when the dawn came found ourselves still on the march, wet and tired and sleepy and bedraggled. Daylight made no difference. On we pressed, climbing a long hill, crowned with plantation buildings and from which we could look down upon a scene of beauty, the green-clad hills and mountains, their tops still wreathed in the morning mist and with no sign that aught but peace and happiness lay in the valleys between them. No time, however, this to enjoy scenery, no matter how picturesque. On we went, now down the hill and into a thick piece of woods, where we halted for a little time, then on again until we once more struck a road and reached El Pozo,

where there had been considerable trouble the day before. Without waiting for us the quadrille had already opened. During our halt in the woods we could hear the artillery and the rifles and soon after we reached the El Pozo road and once more swinging to the right started for San Juan we realized that it might be a case of El Caney over again, for we encountered a steady stream of wounded men going or being carried to the rear. Down the road screeched the Mausers, but still high over our heads and in the distance we could hear the boom of the guns of the Spanish forts as they answered our light artillery. Still onward, with no band or field music to give us the cadenced step, a minute's halt now and then until we were compelled to leave the road to make way for a battery banging recklessly along to take another position. Then across a stream and over an open field in full view of the enemy's trenches on the right, passing the battleground of the day before and, under fire by this time, we swung once more to the right and took position on a hill on nearly the extreme right of the American line.

Rolls had been again stripped off and it was expected we would go into action, but the Spaniards had been given pretty nearly all the fight they wanted that day and there was little for the Second to do but to take its position and stay there. For hours the men lay on the hill crest under the blazing sun, without a chance at cooking a meal and hard pressed for water until details were sent back to the stream with canteens. Sharpshooters made this mission dangerous but no one refused to go.

It was not until early in the evening that the firing died down and it was safe to stand erect and walk about. The rolls and haversacks had been brought up and having been better guarded from prowling Cubans this time the contents of the haversacks were intact. By the time darkness came on the hillside on which we were camped for the day, tents had by this time been put up, was illuminatad by the cooking fires and once more we enjoyed something that would pass for a meal. This over, sleep was the next necessity and we were not long in seeking our downy couches.

But we did not slumber long. Just about 10 o'clock there was a disturbance of the peace by the Spaniards, who apparently wished to spoil the good time we were having. Three or four big guns boomed out and then came the, by this time familiar sound of the Mausers. It needed no bell boy to awake us. In a jiffy we were up and scrambling for rifles and cartridge belts. Then came quickly spoken orders to "fall in" from the company commanders and the voices of the hurrying non-coms as they rounded up the men. All was black darkness and men stumbled over the grass and roots or slipped on the steep hillside. It was a scene of the utmost din and confusion, orders coming fast and loud, the men, still sleep-blinded, hustling about in confusion, the night's stillness broken by the crash of the Spanish rifles and the noise of exploding shells over our heads while on our right we heard the whip-like crack of the Krags answering the Mausers. "Hell's broken loose," avowed a B man as he groped about for his cartridge belt and indeed it seemed so.

Our battalion had its "shacks" on the top of the hill just below the crest while the other companies were scattered all along the hill but further below, so that the men of the Springfield companies were not long in falling in and making their way to the crest. But even then they were not quick enough to satisfy Major Van Horn, the choleric commander of the 22d, who appeared to have as bad a case of what was known to the boys as the "rattles" as any man ever had. Brandishing his sword, he ran about the hill, cursing the Second and ordering every man to the front, although it would have seemed he had enough to do to look after his own outfit. Col. Clark and his officers and the regiment were already on the top of the hill and awaiting events, but for some time Major Van Horn pranced and reared and vented his spleen upon the few men who happened to be a bit slow about getting up until finally his senses returned and he went where he belonged.

All in all our officers and men acted with coolness, considering the circumstances. It is not pleasant or conducive to coolness of thought or action to be suddenly pulled out of bed after a day of great exertion and hustle around in black darkness to the accompaniment of rifle bullets and bombshells and especially when it is uncertain whether the enemy is in one's front, flank or rear and go stumbling up a steep hill so that it is small wonder if at the outset a few were "rattled." But in a very short time, the lines were formed on the top of the hill and the Second waited.

It was fortunate that none of our officers lost their heads and ordered their men to fire for the results could not fail to have been unfortunate all around. Just below us were three of our own regiments and had the Second fired the bullets would have hit our own men. It was a wonder that in the darkness and confusion nothing of the kind was done but officers and men kept their heads well and after the first confused rush up the hill all acted with commendable coolness.

But if we did not use our rifles the enemy did theirs and before the affair was over two men of the Second had been hit, one of them, Private Robert G. Kelly of G. mortally. A Mauser struck him in the left cheek, passing through and severing the lingual artery, lodged in the muscles of the right jaw. The other man hit was Private Peter N. White of A company, whose wound was not serious.

Poor Kelly was taken to his tent, where he lay in agony all night, the surgeons and hospital stewards doing all they could to relieve him. The next morning he was taken to the division hospital near Siboney where he lingered until July 7th, when he died. There was a story, which has never been denied, that his death was caused by internal hemorrhage caused by the imperfect manner in which his wound was cared for in the hospital.

The affair lasted about an hour and when the attacking force of Spaniards had been pretty well cut to pieces the enemy retired within his lines once more and the Second returned to its slumbers. At 3 A. M. there was some more firing but this was merely an affair of outposts and lasted but a few moments, just long enough to break up sleep for the second time that night.

Next day was Sunday, but it could hardly be called a peaceful one. From daybreak to early in the afternoon the sharpshooters of the enemy were active and a man had to walk humbly and keep well under cover unless he cared to make a target of himself. Many of these sharpshooters were inside our lines, not having had an opportunity to get to their own when their companions were driven back and hidden in thick foliaged trees and supplied with rations and water and plenty of ammunition they managed to make matters rather lively for us. Early in the day many squads were sent out to locate and capture these fellows but though many were located few were brought in as prisoners.

Time wore on slowly that Sunday. About noon orders were promulgated that an armistice had been declared and that firing on both sides was to cease at 12 o'clock. This was not bad news but evidently all our Spanish friends did not hear of it until later, for up to 2 o'clock there was an occasional bullet sent toward us from the outlying trenches. After that hour it was possible to walk about without having to dodge.

Early that morning we heard the distance-dulled boom of heavy guns from the direction of the mouth of the harbor. We knew that Sampson and Schley were outside waiting for Cervera and his ships but we had heard the guns of our fleet so often that we supposed it was simply another case of throwing a few shot at the Morro or the other Spanish batteries. Gradually the roar of the guns grew fainter and fainter until they died away altogether and it was supposed the attack of the fleet had again been fruitless. But soon after noon the "JoJo" department got at work again and rumors began to circulate that this time the fleet had been successful and had forced its way past the batteries and into the harbor.

It was not until soon after 4 o'clock that afternoon, however, that we learned what had happened. Then we saw Major Webb of Shafter's staff riding up to our brigade headquarters, which were only a few yards away from Col. Clark's "shack." The major reined up, said a few words to Gen. Ludlow and the latter hastily summoned the regimental commanders and announced that the Spanish fleet had tried to cut its way out of the harbor and had been met by Schley's ships and destroyed. It did not take long for the good news to spread and then such cheering as went up. Hats went up into the air and there was general jubilation. For once the "JoJo" department had been outdone. All along our line we could hear the cheering and then what few regimental bands we had broke loose and gave a jubilee concert which was highly appreciated. We had no religious services that day but the bands played, "There'll be a hot time in Old Town to-night,"

Discipline was relaxed after the armistice had been declared and the men wandered along the lines, visiting other regiments and going over the battlegrounds of the two days previous. Many visited the outposts and took a look at the city and the forts. We could see the Spaniards taking life easy in their trenches and we wondered if they had heard what had happened to their fleet. Some of our boys, disgusted with their Springfields, went "grafting" Krags and picked up a good number, together with plenty of ammunition. Had the entire regiment been turned loose there is no question but what every man would have replaced his Springfield with a Krag-Jorgensen and as it was nearly 150 were obtained and a corresponding number of Sprinfields thrown away.

Our sleep was unbroken that night and we were ready to celebrate July 4th the next morning. Our celebration took the form of a little excursion, for soon after our frugal breakfast we were on the march again and began our celebrated swing to the right with the object of encircling the city. Our brigade led the advance as it had from the start and after four hours of slow progress we swung to the left and took our position on the now famous "Misery hill," an elevation in rear of the city and overlooking it. From the crest we could plainly see the Spanish batteries and barracks, while almost directly in front of us were the hospital buildings with half a dozen Red Cross flags flying over them. We passed our Fourth of July quietly enough. Not a fire cracker was fired, principally because we did not have any and there was not even a rifle crack to mark the day. Late in the afternoon we heard the guns of the fleet again as they hammered away at the harbor batteries for awhile. We pitched our "day tents" and took notice of the fact that our rations were getting low again. Next day we were put at work for the first time digging trenches and we enjoyed the job. For tools there were in the entire regiment only a few shovels and picks but the trenches had to be dug and the boys went at it with their mess knives, spoons and tin plates. It was fierce work under the blazing sun and the soil was hard to dig, but the work was done by reliefs and by night of the next day the trenches of our battalion were completed and good ones they were, too. They were dug on the crest of the hill and were deep enough with the earth parapet to give us protection from anything the enemy might send over at us. They were wide enough to enable the men to move about and the earth was cut away at the rear so as to make a sort of seat. More trouble was anticipated at any moment and ammunition in plenty was placed along the trenches. In fact, there was more ammunition than rations about all the time during the campaign.

Capron's battery, which was with us at El Caney, came up the 6th and took a position on the left of our line of trenches. The digging of intrenchments for this battery afforded us our first opportunity of seeing Cubans work and certainly they did work under Capt. Capron. Other regiments kept coming up and taking positions on our left and the circle about Santiago began to tighten.

Meanwhile we had leisure to lie about and figure up our losses. Malone of B, shot at El Caney, had died in the field hospital the evening of July 2d and his death came as a shock to his friends in that company. Richmond of G died in the same hospital early the preceding evening and that made five good men in the three Springfield companies slain by Spanish bullets. There were many missing faces from the ranks, too, and we kept hearing rumors that this or that man wounded at Caney had died in the hospital. Besides we knew some exaggerated stories about the losses of the Second had gone home and we knew the anxiety which our friends and relatives in Springfield must be feeling.

There were other losses aside from the bullets of the enemy. On July 6th Major Southmayd and Capt. McDonald left camp, the former going home on sick leave and the latter having injured himself badly in the spine. He was accompanied to the hospital by First Sergeant Burke, who remained with him until he sailed for the United States. In Capt. McDonald's absence First Lieut. W. L. Young took command of B company. Capt. John J. Leonard of G was made acting major of Major Southmayd's battalion and retained the command to the close of the campaign. The command of K company devolved upon First Lieut. Phillip C. Powers and First Lieut. W. C. Hayes took command of G company.

About this time many of our boys got "next" to a species of poison vine somewhat resembling the poison ivy of New England and with about the same results. The surgeons could find nothing to counteract the effects of the vine until a Cuban told them of another plant which being steeped was an effective antidote for the poison and a free use of this soon restored the swollen faces and hands of the sufferers to their normal condition.

"Misery hill" was a delightful place especially when the rations began to get shy as they did soon after our arrival. The visits of the pack train were few and far between and it was just as likely as not to bring ammunition instead of rations. Issues of one or two hardtack and a thin slice of bacon for a twenty-four hours ration were common, and some of the boys supplemented their menu with mangoes and "monkey plumes." Sergeant Lovely of G enjoyed the distinction of eating twenty-four mangoes in one day, much to the horror of the surgeons when they heard of it, but with no bad results to him.

It was while we were on "Misery hill" that "Dido" Hunt achieved added fame by his abilities as a butcher. Gen. Ludlow had a desire for beefsteak and had purchased a hungry looking cow from some Cubans, Private Hunt as regimental butcher, being detailed to kill the animal. It was just before dusk, one evening, when the cow was led forth to the slaughter and "Dido," armed with a revolver, got ready to act as executioner. He fired again and again at the cow, the animal after each shot, looking about in a surprised manner as if wondering what the racket was all about. Finally one of the bullets hit the cow somewhere, and with a bellow of pain and fright, she ran off and disappeared in the darkness, leaving Private Hunt and the man who had been holding the rope gazing at each other. Gen. Ludlow had no steak that evening and the fate of the cow was never learned although there were rumors that the animal had ended her career in the camp of one of the regular regiments, the men of which had a fresh meat supper that night.

A "commissary" had been established near Siboney by some enterprising sutlers, and the company officers were enabled to purchase some tea, oatmeal, etc., for their men. These were especially valuable, as several had succumbed to the climate and the toil and exposure of the campaign, and the hardtack and bacon were not the best kind of food for them. About this time, too, we were threatened with an outbreak of measles, but the cases were promptly isolated and the disease did not spread.

CHAPTER XIV.

WE CONTINUE OUR EDUCATION IN THE ART OF WAR AND LEARN A FEW THINGS.

OUR stay on "Misery hill" lasted just seven days and in that time we learned a few things, the art of trench digging without intrenching tools, standing out in our memory as one most important lesson. We learned how to sleep on a side hill without our bodies slipping entirely out from the shelter tents during our slumbers, this being accomplished by the simple means of driving a couple of pegs into the ground at the opening of the tent and placing a stick against them, our feet resting against the stick and preventing us going any further. We acquired the art of making cigarettes and of using anything at all in the paper line to roll them in. The inner pith of the royal palm came in handily for this purpose when our supply of cigarette paper gave out. We learned how to make one match light several pipes or cigarettes, for matches were scarce and therefore not to be wasted. We learned how to make the brook water passably cool in our canteens, by thoroughly soaking the canvass covering of the canteen and then suspending it from a tree or tent pole, the evaporation of the moisture of the cover slowly cooling the contents. At night the canteens were hung from the tent poles and in the morning the water was usually quite cool. Later on long branches of bamboo were used as water vessels and one trip to the brook usually sufficed for the day. In the building of "shacks" by which the regulars who had served in the west designated about everything in the way of a shelter from the sun or rain, we obtained lessons from our friends of the 8th and 22d. A couple of crotched sticks across which was laid a center pole formed the usual frame work of the structure and the roof and sides were composed of bushes or palm leaves. These were more airy than our tents and more comfortable except when it rained heavily.

Also, we learned to do without stockings, the fact being that the bulk of our hosiery was either worn out or thrown away, and we took a card from the regulars and discarded such things in the line thereof, greasing our feet with the luscious "sow belly." In laundry work we became expert. "Jim" Ryan's steam laundry had long since gone into voluntary bankruptcy, and every man was his own laundryman. Insect enemies began to appear, and obtained a lodgment in spite of strenuous efforts. Soap was scarce and there were times when water was not the easiest thing in the world to get. Our sleeping arrangements were primitive, the usual method of arranging them being to place the rubber blanket on the ground with the coated side down, on this place the woolen blanket and wrapping this about us, go to sleep. Our coats, or shoes, or anything else suitable, being utilized for pillows. While on "Misery hill" many of the boys cut grass and utilized it as mattresses, but we could not do this on our short bivouacs.

As to cooking, we were "stars." That is when there was anything to cook. On these occasions our culinary preparations were delightfully simple and even chafing-dish outfits would have to bow to our superior ingenuity. Our cooking apparatus required a small fire of wood, and the utensils were all carried in our haversacks. They were a combined frying pan and plate of tin, the former having a handle, a sharp pointed knife, fork and spoon. The basis of our menu was especially noticeable for its simplicity, the staples being bacon, hardtack, canned tomatoes and coffee. Sometimes we had sugar and more times we didn't. Occasionally we had a bit of salt or pepper and on these rare occasions there was joy, for then we were enabled to make the stuff labelled "canned roast beef" palatable enough so that it could be forced down our throats. At other times, Ugh! If the devil hasn't a special corner in the hot room of his Turkish bath reserved for those responsible for that "canned roast beef," he isn't "onto his job."

Even with such simple means we managed to vary the menus a bit at times. Our usual breakfast was bacon and hardtack and coffee. The bacon was usually without a bit of lean and after frying for a moment or two the pan was about half-filled with fat, leaving a shrivelled up and brittle piece of so-called bacon. But it was eaten just the same, our stomachs having been educated up to anything. Sometimes we fried our hardtack in the bacon grease and these with black coffee, sometimes without sugar, made up our breakfast. Thanks to a beneficent government we had coffee about all the time, if we had nothing else. It came to us in the berry, in paper packages, and our chief concern as to coffee was how to grind or pulverize it. Usually this was done by the simple but slow process of putting a few berries in our tin cups and pounding them with a stick or tent pole until they were broken enough to steep. Then the cup was filled with water and placed in the fire until the coffee boiled when the cup was taken out by means of a cleft stick or a bayonet and laid aside to cool sufficiently to drink. There was plenty of barbed wire everywhere and by means of the wire cutters rude grates were made on which the tin cup was placed. For dinner the bill of fare and the method of preparing it was about the same, likewise for supper. Sometimes, when we had canned tomatoes we made "sludge," a simple confection of tomatoes and broken hardtack, with at times a few "strings" of the corned beef thrown in to give it, not taste, but more body. This "beef" was also used to form the groundwork for an imitation stew, the only resemblance to stew being the name, for it was without onions or potatoes. Then we made "Santiago sludge cakes," composed of pulverized hardtack and water, the mixture being patted into cakes and fried in bacon grease. Sometimes a bit of sugar was sprinkled over them, and we deluded ourselves into the belief that we were eating something very fine. Another method of preparing this delicacy was to mix in some canned tomato. Mango stew we had at times, but not often, as sugar was scarce.

Gout might fairly have been expected as the result of this high living, (we were camped on a hill,) but, strange to say, no cases were reported, and even dyspepsia was unknown. Our regular hours doubtless aided us in keeping off these two diseases. We were aroused by reveille very early in the morning, usually about dawn and retired early in the evening. It grew dark about 8 o'clock and by that time everyone but the sentries was in quarters and usually asleep.

The personal appearance of our officers and men was not as prepossessing as it might have been. Coats and collars were not *de rigeur* and the only headgear was very "bum" looking campaign hats. Usually our blue shirts were open at the neck and a blue handkerchief carelessly knotted *a la* cow boy was our only ornament. Suspenders were viewed with suspicion and the cartridge belts, with their thimbles filled with ammunition, served also the purpose of keeping our trousers up. These trousers were showing the wear and tear of the campaign, and needed pressing badly, being also used for pajamas. Our leggings were mostly torn and frayed, and went well with the trousers so far as looks were concerned, as for shoes, they too had seen better days. Barbers were at a discount and full beards were popular, the most noticeable ones in the three Springfield companies being those of Lieuts. Powers and Parkhurst of K, and Sergeants Scully and Murphy of G, although Gardella's was not far behind.

In K "Bert" Nichols and "Ad" Potter had trained down so fine that their bodies failed to cast a shadow, and "Billy" Fish had got down to less than 200 pounds. The beard possessed by Morris Greenowitz of B was nearly all that remained of him and Jack Fulton was travelling in the same road. Alberts of B was having a good time with the horses and the Chaplain, and in K the Turner brothers were having hourly arguments with each other on the relative nutritious qualities of canned roast and corned beef. "Wap" Packard of G was busy figuring how many men were by his brother's side when he was shot, and had already counted up 35 with several more districts to hear from, and "Jim" Shene of the same company was planning foraging expeditions with Private Mahoney of Mittineague. "Batty" Hayes had secured a divorce from "Marguerite" Gelinas and was busy trying to keep the case out of the papers.

So the days passed on "Misery hill" until noon of the 10th, when we were ordered to move on, once more to the right, and we left our fine trenches only to have them occupied by the 71st New York, the "heroes" of San Juan. We halted after a couple of hours, there being some trenches dug by Garcias Cubans, and occupied them at 4 o'clock when our batteries opened upon Santiago. The affair lasted until 6, but the enemy's reply was not very loud and we did not get a chance to use our Springfields.

Next morning we were on the march again, and this time it lasted about all day, up hill and down hill, until just before dusk we halted for the night with the right of our brigade resting on the Cobre road, thus cutting off the last avenue of escape from the city for the Spaniards, and the only way by which reinforcements from Holguin or the rest of the province could be put into the city. Rumors that a large

Spanish force was on the way, made us vigilant and our guards were instructed to keep the sharpest kind of a watch, but as events proved, it was not necessary. Hardly had the boys got their tents up and their supper cooked, before the mail came up, and such a rush as there was for it. We had received one mail from home while on "Misery hill," and every man who failed to receive a letter then, was certain there was one or more for him now and could hardly wait to have the contents of the sacks distributed.

That night we had to take off our hats to the Cuban rain storm. Hardly had the mail been distributed when it began to rain. Up to this what rain there was had usually fallen in the afternoon and was not of long duration, but the rain of July 11th and 12th will be remembered by every one in the Fifth Army Corps. It came down all night in solid sheets and our shelter tents and rubber blankets were of little use against it. When morning came everybody and everything was drenched, and a more forlorn looking outfit can hardly be imagined. About 6 A. M., the rain ceased for an hour or two and as soon as possible huge fires of bamboo were blazing and the men essayed to dry themselves and their clothing and to cook breakfast. Fortunately there was plenty of bamboo near our camp, and the wood burned as well wet as dry. But it was not long before down came the rain again just as bad as during the night, and to add to our discomfort, came orders to pack up and move on again.

Rolling up our saturated tents and blankets, and wet to the skin, we took up the march and after wading through the deep mud of the Cobre road for a short distance, plunged into a trail which would take us to our new position and our last camp in Cuba. But it was not long before we found that the trail led through a piece of swampy ground, and before they had gone far the boys found themselves up to their legging tops in mud and the ooze of the swamp. It took a long time to flounder along through this, but it was finally done and the regiment emerged upon firm ground, and was soon on the spot selected for its occupancy.

All this time the rain kept on, and it was not until nearly 4 P. M., that it ceased and the sun came out. Meanwhile, the well soaked shelter tents had been put up and the men were either huddled under them and saying things about the wet season and Cuba, or were standing about with their rubber blankets thrown over their heads. But with the coming of the sun there was a great change. Its rays were so fierce that within half an hour there was scarcely any indication that it had been raining all night and all day, the ground dried up rapidly and so did the shelter tents. Off came the rubber blankets from the men, and clothing and equipments were spread out to dry in the afternoon sun. Wood was hustled for and with the blaze of the cooking fires and the smell of bacon and coffee cheerfulness returned.

That evening the boys were put at work again digging trenches. Up to this Gen. Toral had hesitated to respond to Shafter's invitation to come out and surrender and the arrival of Gen. Miles having stiffened up the latter gentleman's backbone, some more trouble was looked for. Our brigade was, as usual, on the extreme right of the American line and the 8th regiment lay directly opposite the head of the harbor, the 22d next and then "ours." Right in front of our center and less than 500 yards away was the bull ring of Santiago, a circular wooden building filled with Spanish soldiers, while in front of that we could see the trenches with the soldiers lounging about, and with a glass could discern the barbed wire fencing and entanglements in front of the trenches. Our position was an exposed one, for from their position the enemy could have raked us front and flank, so at the trenches we went under the direction of Major Whipple.

By this time our regiment had been supplied with a fairly decent number of intrenching tools and the boys, appreciating the necessity for trenches, went at the work with but lit-

tle grumbling. The trenches were dug on three sides of a square, one in front of each battalion, the work being done by each company in relays. Major Whipple's battalion now had the right, Major Fairbanks' the center and ours the left, so that it was in the rear of the other two. The work was continued to a late hour that night, and all the next day, and finished on the morning of the 14th. The trenches were even better than those dug on "Misery hill" and were complimented by Gen. Ludlow, who was a colonel of engineers before he became a general of volunteers. Not to be behind hand the non-commissioned staff of the regiment and the headquarters attaches dug a trench for themselves and the regiment was ready for the next move.

Twelve o'clock at noon of the 24th was the hour set for the ending of the truce, and at 11.30 A. M. we were ordered into the trenches. Everyone felt there was going to be a hard fight this time, for it was considered certain that the enemy would make a determined resistance and our estimate of Spanish valor had gone up many degrees since El Caney. It was known that an assault by the Americans was to follow the bombardment and those who had noted the enemy's preparations for defense knew that we were in for a warm reception and that if we charged up to the barbed wire entanglements and the trenches many would not return. But that made little difference and we took our position in the trenches and waited for the opening gun from Capron's battery, posted on a hill in our rear. The horses and the Chaplain had gone to the rear and the surgeons and hospital corps were posted in readiness for what might happen. Hardly had we got into the trenches when the buzzards began to gather, and this to us was a certain indication of a battle.

Noon came and the white flag of truce still waved from the governor's palace and the signal gun was not fired. Half after 12 and no change. We wondered what was up.

Nothing much could be seen from the trenches and nearly all of the boys climbed to the top and sat down with eager eyes fastened upon the city we were going to capture. One o'clock and the white flag still floated. Now came the "Jo Jo" department to the front once again, and the news ran from trench to trench, that Shafter had postponed the assault and given the Spaniards a few days more in which to make up their mind. Following this came the information that Gen. Toral was merely trying to gain time in order that 10,000 Spanish troops which were coming up, might attack us in the rear while Toral's men sallied out in our front. And then down came the rain in large and continuous sheets, soon flooding the trenches and making us forget the impending battle, "Jo Jo's," and everything else but the necessity of keeping as dry as possible. The rain lasted for an hour and a half, filling our lovely trenches with water and putting them in nice shape for a battle. But hardly had the sun reappeared before we saw a horseman clad in the Khaki uniform of Shafter's staff galloping along the lines toward us and in his wake we saw the hats of the men in the trenches being thrown into the air, and the wearers dancing as if some extra good news had come. Reining up in front of the center trench where Col. Clark was, the horseman gave him the welcome news that the city had surrendered, and as the constantly increasing knot of officers and men who had got within earshot, began to get ready for a vocal demonstration, the aide added, "Orders are not to cheer, boys, for the deal isn't quite fixed up, but you can throw your hats into the air all you wish." Well, the boys followed instructions and the hats went up, while the aide dashed over to the 8th and 22d with the news.

And it was good news. It meant no more trench digging, no more marching, no more fighting, and last but not least, as some of our long headed and practical ones figured it out, it meant more and varied rations, for now our ships could come into the harbor. The trenches were quickly emptied and we returned to our shacks in pretty good spirits.

It was not until three days after, on Sunday the 17th. that the formal surrender took place. The troops were assembled in front of their trenches, and as the gun announcing the hoisting of our flag over the governor's palace, boomed out, we cheered, and then marched back only to be formed in front of Col. Clark's quarters, where certain men were given a "wigging" which they remembered for a long time. Since the 14th our men had been allowed to go freely outside our lines, and although not permitted to go into the city proper, yet they found some interesting things in the suburbs. One of these was the cemetery and some regulars and a number of Second men had gone there and thoughtlessly taken some flowers and trinkets from some graves. This desecration had been reported by the Spaniards to Gen. Shafter and the latter "wigged" Gen. Lawton about it. Lawton repeating the operation to Gen. Ludlow and the latter giving Col. Clark and the commanding officer of the 22d a bad quarter of an hour. So when it came his turn, Col. Clark let himself out on the men, and his remarks were of the keen and cutting style which makes a man feel good when he hears some other fellow getting them. This concluded the exercises of the day and we were dismissed to think it over,

Next day the "Jo Jo" bureau resumed operations and we heard "on the best of authority," of course, that we were to be hustled on to Porto Rico with Gen. Miles. Next came the news that our brigade, having done so well was to be sent against Holguin in the interior of the province where there were some 8000 Spanish troops, who had been surrendered with those in Santiano but did not like it and proposed to fight. Within the next few days it was gravely announced by the "Jo Jo," that we were going to be sent to the Philippines, as experienced and acclimated troops were wanted there; that we were to be sent to help capture Havana, marching from Santiago for that purpose, and best of all, that unless Spain sued for peace within a week, we were to embark for that country and invade it. As to the "Jo Jos" about double pay, the receipt by each man of a lump sum of money in consideration of waiving our claims to a pension, etc., they were numerous and varied enough to fill a large book. In its "Jo Jo" bureau the Second had some distinguished artists.

But the most convincing sign of all that the city had surrendered, was the arrival of rations, and they were gladly received. For a day or two it was the familiar bacon and hardtack, but soon we were surprised and gladdened by the sound of mule wagons coming up the road from the city and laden with good looking loaves of soft bread. We then found that army ovens had been established in the city and that we would have bread in abundance. Next came some refrigerated beef, and it looked good and tasted better. Our first issue of the beef was quickly disposed of, each man's share being taken to the nearest fire and a "bluff" made at broiling it, the majority of the men being too "meat hungry" to do more than merely toast it. That first "beefsteak supper" of ours on the island is remembered yet. Next day came more beef, more bread and finally potatoes and onions, while with them were brought along rice and canned tomatoes and bacon and hardtack. The two latter we scorned. Eat hardtack and canned beef when we had fresh bread and meat and the materials for beef stew? Well, we guessed not. But it turned out we were too proud. There came days when the refrigerated beef became less relished, especially when our noses could learn of its being on the way long before it reached the camp, and we were glad to fall back on the despised, "sowbelly," and by this time in deference to our luxurious tastes, the conscience stricken commissary department was sending us something that resembled bacon far more than anything we had previously had, and that came in nice tin packages. Even the soft bread palled on us after a while, and we were glad to nibble a hardtack now and then, especially, when as sometimes happened the bread was sour.

A few days after the surrender, B company was gladdened by the arrival of its cook, Walter Butler, who had remained on the ship and who, on his arrival, took charge of the culinary department and began to concoct some excellent stews. The Buzzicot field-cooking outfits, which we had brought from Massachusetts with us, were also landed, and that of G was at once set up with Private Carl Mueller as cook and Corporal "Nat" Gardella and "Dido" Hunt as steward and assistant steward, and "Daniel" Bellamy, the well-known temperance orator, as chief of the wood and water department. Private Fisher, the company cook of K, was ill, and K's Buzzicot was but little used.

The day after our arrival in this camp, Private Bates of K severely injured his foot while chopping wood, the axe slipping and severing one of the arteries. He was laid up for some days.

G and K moved their camps to the other side of the trenches about the 20th, but B remained where it was. The wall tents which we brought with us from South Framingham and used at Lakeland and Tampa, also came up, and at once took the place of the "pup tents" we had used on the island. Our knapsacks and other property which we left on the Knickerbocker were also sent to us and we found that some of our things were left, although many knapsacks which had been left well filled, on the boat, had been "touched."

Once again we began to have the same old shortage of rations, and this time with our ships in the harbor we couldn't understand it. One day we received two hardtack and a spoonful of coffee berries for a twenty-four hours issue. We were out of fresh meat, sugar and everything else, but this only lasted a couple of days and then we got fresh meat, vegetables and beans.

CHAPTER XV.

WE HAVE TO FACE ANOTHER ENEMY MORE DEADLY THAN THE SPANIARDS.

AND now that the Spaniards had been conquered and Santiago was ours we found ourselves facing another enemy even more deadly than the Mauser bullets or the machette. Up to the surrender the health of our regiment, everything considered, had been fairly good. Sickness there was to be sure, but nothing more than was to be expected in a regiment of 900 men subjected to the exposures and hardships incidental to a campaign in a foreign land, and these exposures supplemented by a ration, which even when plentiful, which was not often, was entirely unfitted for soldiers campaigning in a warm climate. Again it must be remembered that our work in Cuba was performed in the rainy season and that sleeping in mud, marching and bivouacking in the rain and fording deep streams are not conducive to rugged health when persisted in day after day. But so long as the active campaign lasted, the excitement and novelty of it all kept the men up. After the surrender, when there was little or nothing for them to do, they were in condition to fall an easy prey to the "calentura" or malarial fever, and to the diseases of the stomach incident to camp life with a poorly adapted ration. Fat bacon and canned beans, containing fully as much grease as beans, are not the kind of food the sensible man going to spend a time in the tropics would select for his menu, but that is what we got and it was eat it or nothing.

During the active campaign many men of the regiment were ill from one cause or another, but as a matter of fact, there was nothing like a general outbreak of sickness at any time until some days after the surrender. A number of the men contracted rheumatism from sleeping on the damp ground and there were scattered cases of measles and stomach disorders. But the average daily sick report never went much beyond a dozen cases, which it must be admitted is not bad for an organization of nearly 1000 men living under the conditions which we did.

For the first few days after Santiago surrendered all went well. There were propositions to move the troops further inland and up into the mountains with a view of escaping any possibility af the dreaded yellow fever which was showing itself at Siboney, the houses of which village had been burned to the ground in order to remove the danger of infection, but the contemplated move was not made and we remained in our last station until the regiment sailed for Montauk Point.

On the day after the surrender Col. Clark issued orders for daily company drills and inspections with a view of giving the men something to do, he recognizing, as an old soldier, that idleness is the worst possible thing in camp. He and his superiors realized, however, that the army had passed through a most trying, though short campaign, and that the men deserved a rest, but at the same time there were already warnings that the less active the men were, the easier they fell prey to the climatic diseases of the country. Even after we had been in our last camp for a few days, there were signs that the fever was at work and with our limited supply of medicines, it was feared that it might become epidemic. That these fears were only too well grounded was soon to be made manifest.

The day following the surrender, Col. Clark and Major

Bowen, the regimental surgeon, established a hospital in an old and dilapidated wooden building a couple of hundred yards in front of our advanced line of trenches and which had been used as a railway station. It was in poor shape, the roof being partly gone and the flooring bad, but it was better than leaving the sick men in their stuffy little shelter tents or out in the open air. The division hospitals were already overcrowded with wounded and sick men and the regimental commanders were notified that they would have to care for their own sick as best they could. Even as bad as the building selected for our hospital was, it was looked upon with envy by the commanding officers of other regiments and it was even suggested to Col. Clark that he divide it up with the other regiments of our brigade.

Whether it was the camping along the line of the recently made trenches, the earth of which was said to be full of malarial germs, or that the fever was already in the air that caused the epidemic among our men is not certain, but within a day or two after the Sunday on which the Stars and Stripes were hoisted over the city the fever began its career in our regiment and in a few days over fifty per cent. of the officers and men were affected with it. The daily drills soon had to be discontinued, for hardly enough men to make a decent showing were able to turn out for them in the majority of the companies. It was the same way at the daily inspections. Frequently a man standing in the ranks would fall down in his tracks from sheer weakness and would have to be carried to his tent by his comrades. Soon there was no pretence of conforming to the orders requiring these drills and inspections and the men, who were able to move at all, did so as if their feet were encased in lead. At surgeon's call every morning there were sights which were enough to appall the stoutest hearted among us. It was directly after reveille that this call was sounded, and then from all parts of the camp dreary processions of what had been strong and hearty looking young men, would drag themselves slowly to the surgeon's tent and stand or lie on the ground waiting for their turn to be treated. And it must be said that the treatment was not of a sort calculated to cheer them up. The only medicines on hand were quinine and salts and a preparation for stomach disorders. Of quinine there was a plenty, but after a time the systems of the men, in many cases, became so saturated with it that even doses of thirty grains or more produced but little effect. And what hurt the boys more than the fever or anything else was the feeling, right or wrong as it may have been, that we of the Fifth Army Corps, who had done our work uncomplainingly, and done it well, were being neglected by the government whose call we had obeyed among the first. It was known that our state had sent us away from South Framingham with a medicine chest second to none in the army, and that this chest was even now on board of one of the transports in the harbor, but for all practical uses, as far off as the North Pole. Some of us knew that requisition after requisition for medical supplies had been sent in by our surgeon and had not been honored, that in spite of all our surgeons and stewards could do it was next to an impossibility to obtain an ambulance, and that we were even denied the services of one of our assistant surgeons, Dr. Gates having been detailed to the Fourth infantry, which was at that time without a medical officer,

All these things helped the fever. Depression was its best ally, and then came nostalgia, the homesickness which men who have never experienced sneer at, but which is the bane of armies, and which in the Cuban campaign helped kill more men than the bullets of the Spaniards. For nurses for the sick there were only their comrades, willing enough God knows, but unaccustomed to the work, and with their own nerves and tempers wrought up to a high pitch. With lack of surgeons, lack of medicines, lack of nurses, lack of proper food, lack of proper accommodations and lack of everything that sick men should have, it is a wonder that the entire regiment was not left behind to fill graves in Cuba.

But even a more pitiful sight than the men who answered the surgeon's call every morning had to witness, was the spectacle of the poor fellows who were unable to get up from their beds on the ground, and who lay there day after day under the stuffy tents, their bodies burning up with the fever, too weak or too despairing to even accept the poor nourishment which their comrades tried to get for them, and in some cases so far gone with nostalgia that they refused everything and only wished for death. It is a known fact that fifty per cent. of the men of the Second who died in that last camp of ours in Cuba, died of nostalgia and nothing else.

Meanwhile, everything that could be done with the limited resources at command, was being done. The company commanders sent into Santiago and bought at the commissary stores, such decent food for sick men as could be procured, and through the efforts of Col. Clark, some suitable food and delicacies were obtained from the Red Cross society. The Colonel also purchased, at his own expense, a number of cots and hammocks for the regimental hospital.

It was indeed a trying time. Officer after officer and man after man went down with the fever. Adjutant Paul R. Hawkins was hard hit with it and was finally removed to the second division hospital. Major Henry C. Bowen, the regimental surgeon, also succumbed and was taken to the same hospital where he died. Quartermaster E. E. Sawtell was another victim but did not go to the hospital. Captain John J. Leonard of G, was stricken and for long days fought the disease in his quarters, and Lieut. Edward J. Leyden of his company was taken to the hospital. Lieut. W. L. Young and Lieut. Harry J. Vesper of B were attacked, the former not seriously, however. There were but few men in any of the companies fit for duty and it was difficult to get enough men for the necessary details. The drills were given up for not enough men to make a decent showing were fit to turn out and it was with difficulty that enough men for regimental and brigade guard were provided. Some necessary work had to be done and from brigade and division headquarters details were constantly being asked for and every man able to stand on his feet had to be pressed into service.

The officers, during this trying time, did all in their power for their men, but it was not much they were able to do and the men felt at the time, that they should have done more. In this they were unjust, for the officers were suffering as much as the men, and the latter have since come to realize that many of the opinions expressed at this time and later, on this subject, were unjust. The fever and the other diseases spared no one, whether he wore shoulder straps or not.

Dr. Hitchcock, our assistant surgeon, succumbed to the fever, and was taken to the division hospital and the surgeon, Dr. Bowen, soon followed him there. This left us without a medical officer, and for two or three days the outlook for the sick men of the Second was a dark one. But we were then provided with two contract surgeons, Dr. Persons and Dr. Dunwoody, and both proved themselves excellent gentlemen and hard workers. Soon after their arrival, Dr. Gates, our other assistant surgeon, who had been detailed to the Fourth infantry, was sent back to us, and his presence was as good as a tonic to the sick men. His cheery smile and sympathetic ways were even better than his medicines, and for a time, after his return, the health of the command appeared to improve. Meanwhile, the famous "round robbin" had been sent, and its result was that the Fifth corps was ordered to return home as soon as transports could be procured. From then until August 12 the thoughts of the men were concentrated upon the time we were to go home.

Meanwhile, the men who escaped the fever and other diseases, were doing all possible for their comrades. The company officers, finding that idleness at this time was the worst possible thing for the men who were at all able to get about, set them at work, and though this seemed at the time a hardship to the men, it turned out to be the best thing that could be done, for it not only served to keep them in better shape physically but helped to keep their minds occupied and prevented them from dwelling too much upon the gloomy situation in the camps and from thinking too much of home. They were encouraged and in most cases ordered to build raised bunks for themselves, these serving to keep their bodies off the ground while sleeping, and to erect shelters of boughs and palm leaves instead of remaining in their shelter tents. When the big wall tents arrived there was no further need of these "shacks" but they served a useful purpose even if not handsome looking.

It was not long after the surrender that we began to get large packages of mail, including the Springfield papers and it is hardly necessary to say that they were welcome. In these papers we found stories of the campaign and of the part the Second had played in the actions at El Caney and San Juan. Many of the letters the boys had written from Tampa and Cuba had been printed and in the reading of these there was much fun. We learned from the papers of the big Fourth of July celebration that had been planned in Springfield, and how it had been given up when the news of El Caney and the rumors of heavy loss in "Ours" reached home. And we received the Fourth of July buttons which had been made in honor of that occasion and proudly wore them about the camp to the envy of some of the other companies of the regiment. It did us some good to know that we had not been entirely forgotten. And sometimes in the mails there were packages for us, sent by loving friends from home and welcome, whether they contained much or little. The arrival of the mail was an event in those days. Sometimes all that there was could be brought from Santiago on the back of one horse, but there were times when one of the two wheeled carretas was necessary to transport it. The array of bags would be dumped off in front of the office tent of the regiment and then the work of sorting out the contents would begin. That destined for each company having been piled up, there were usually enough men waiting to take it away, and for the next few hours the men would read their letters and papers and exchange news. The arrival of the mail was invariably followed by a time of letter writing and the return mail was sometimes nearly as heavy as that which had come in.

As time went on the fever appeared to be wearing itself out and some of those who had it began to recover slowly until they were able to drag themselves around. For days there was a feeling that the worst was over, and this feeling was especially strong in our battalion, which, by the way, had not as yet been as hard hit by the fever as some of the other sections of the regiment. But then came the yellow fever scare and the deaths of one or two of our men and these resulted in a return of the old depression and consequently the sickness.

Quartermaster Sergeant Richard H. Bearse of B, was the first man of the Springfield companies to succumb to the fever and the nostalgia which accompanied it. He was taken sick soon after the surrender, but kept up and about for some time, as he had all through the campaign. But he went down at last and the end came on rapidly. He died on August 1st, and there was not a man in the regiment more regretted for all who ever knew " Dicky " Bearse, loved him.

The second man to go, in the battalion, was Corporal W. C. Piper of K, who died in the division hospital, August 5th, of pernicious malarial fever. He had been taken there only the day before and his comrades were horror stricken when notified of his death. The day following a detail from his company was sent to the hospital and buried him. Private

Paul Vesper of B, died the 10th, from the same cause as Piper, in the division hospital.

It was a day or two afterwards that we heard of the famous "round robin" and its result. The thought of soon sailing for home did much to cheer us up and we began to make what few preparations we had to make, although there was as yet nothing authentic about our going. But on the 10th Col Clark received orders to be ready to embark on short notice and the news spread like wildfire through our camp. Our working suits which we had worn all through the campaign, and our blankets and haversacks were ordered burned and in place of them we were issued the khaki uniforms of yellow with blue facings.

A few days before Col. John F. Marsh, of Springfield, had arrived, and brought with him several boxes of good things sent by the people of Springfield. The time was so short that many of the boxes were unopened and were taken to the ship when we sailed. Nearly all their contents were looted, however, during our trip to Montauk point.

August 11th we received orders to embark the following day, and on the 12th those of the regiment able to march, fell in, and we "hiked the pike" for Santiago. With flags flying we marched through the Calle de Marina, or Marine street, and after a short wait on a pier, were put on a lighter and taken off to the transport Mobile, already occupied by the other two regiments of our brigade and a number of horses. The sick officers and men were sent to the pier in ambulances and those able to walk not only had to do that, but were also obliged to handle all the baggage, a job that would have been child's play at other times, but which in our debilitated condition was a task almost beyond our strength. Col. Clark had been attacked with the fever that morning and was unable to do anything. Lieut. Col. Shumway was so ill as to be unfit for duty but he stuck it out and did what he could. Lieut. Hawkins and Lieut. Leyden were brought down from the division hospital and Lieut. Vesper was brought down from his tent in our camp by Captain Crosier of D. Company.

Meanwhile there were a number of our men sick in their quarters or in the hospitals who could not be moved to the ship, besides others who had been spotted as "suspicious" cases by the surgeons on the day previous, and ordered to remain behind, it being feared that they were in the first stages of yellow fever. It was necessary that some remain behind to care for these poor fellows, but who to detail to this hard duty was a problem which Col. Clark finally solved by detailing Lieut. W. H. Plummer of A. Company of Worcester, and a detail of one man from each company in the regiment to remain. Private Dozilva Lamoreaux of G, Private Robert A. Draper of B and Private Albert Marsden of K volunteered to compose this detail from our companies, and their sacrifices in doing this will not be forgotten by their comrades.

Privates Little, Stetson, Brownell and Dunn of G company, Corporal John B. Fulton, and Privates Judd, Rivers, Champagne, Smith, Wheeler and Frey of B company, and Privates Maynard, Solace and Hall of K were left behind on the island, either sick or as yellow fever suspects when the regiment was ordered home.

1ST TURRET'S CREW. MONITOR LEHIGH.

CHAPTER XVI.

OUR VOYAGE HOMEWARD ON THE DEATH SHIP MOBILE.

OUR voyage homeward on the Mobile was not exactly a pleasant one. At the very outset we again found that in army language we were "up against it." Our entire brigade, composing some 1500 officers and men, were on the boat, which, although large, was not fitted up in very good shape for transport service and as a result there was at first much overcrowding. The Mobile had recently conveyed a cargo of mules to Porto Rico and on her return from that duty had lain for several days in the festering harbor of Santiago so that her sanitary condition could not be termed an ideal one. The officers were crowded together in her few state-rooms and as for the men they were jammed below decks and above decks in any old way. The Eighth and Twenty-second regiments had been on board some time before our regiment arrived and of course had appropriated the best portions of the ship to themselves, something for which they could not be blamed so very much.

That evening we of the Second just simply "bunked" anywhere we could and as a rule we went to bed supperless, for everything was in such a mixed up condition there was no effort made at giving out rations. And on our arrival we found that we were to pass another time with our old friends, the canned "beef" and the nourishing and palatable (!) travel rations. After bidding them farewell, as we thought, forever, this was felt to be the worst blow we had yet suffered but there was no use "kicking" and we made the best of it. Fortunately or unfortunately, as one looks at it, the majority of the men had money enough to purchase quantities of canned fruits and delicacies before they left Santiago and these helped us out to some extent.

What we at first thought was a blessing but which afterward turned out to be the reverse was the presence of a large tank of ice water below decks to which we freely helped ourselves and with evil effect upon some of the men who developed dysentery from indulging too freely in the cold liquid. After a day or two the ice water was shut off from the men, and they were compelled to drink the regular ship's water. There was any amount of grumbling at this but it was the best thing to be done under the circumstances.

We remained in the harbor the night of the 12th and early on the 13th, our old "hoodoo" number being with us again, the Mobile swung her nose around and steamed down the harbor. Every man able to be up was on deck as we started out and realized that we were homeward bound at last. There were mighty few regrets expressed at leaving Cuba and our chief concern now was to reach home as quickly as possible. It was known that our destination was Montauk Point, L. I., and beyond that our information was a trifle hazy.

Passing down the harbor we came to the Merrimac as she lay about where Hobson had sunk her and we could see that she was not of much avail in stopping the channel. A little further we passed the wreck of the Reina Mercedes as she lay where the shells from our warships had put her out of business and just a little distance further along we passed out under the frowning walls and grim looking guns of Castle Morro, over which our flag was now floating. On the other side of the harbor entrance was an unimportant looking sand battery, but it was from it that the Spanish guns did their most effective work against our fleet. One turn more and we were out of the harbor and again on the bounding billows.

This day quarters were assigned the various companies of our regiment below decks. The men were supplied with hammocks and as these had to be slung close together and the men were just a bit unfamiliar with their management there were many tumbles out of bed that night. We found the sleeping accommodations on the Mobile suberb. If you say that word "superb" quick it sounds well and that's the way we said it. A number of the men were obliged to sleep on deck and under a covering of loose planks and as it happened to rain two or three nights in succession, they did not like their sleeping quarters any too well.

The steward of the Mobile was an Englishman, like all her officers, and he was a direct descendant of thieves and inherited all their instincts of robbery. He thought nothing of charging $5 for a half-pint of vile liquor and his prices for anything else he could sell were in proportion. He contracted with some of the company commanders to furnish a number of loaves of bread each day for the men but the loaves turned out to be nothing more than biscuits and the prices asked were so exorbitant that a complaint was made to the captain of the ship and the steward was compelled to make restitution.

One of the first incidents of our passage homeward was the stopping of the Mobile by a United States gunboat on our second evening out from Santiago harbor. It seems that the Mobile was not showing just the proper lights and the gunboat steamed close to her to investigate, firing a blank charge across her bows as a signal to stop. The Mobile stopped. Then after a brief colloquy between the little gunboat and the big Mobile the latter was allowed to proceed. It should be said, however, that when the officers and crew of the gunboat ascertained that the Second Massachusetts was on board they gave us three hearty cheers.

Life on board the Mobile was not a bit more luxurious than it had been on the Knickerbocker or in Cuba. We had the same old travel rations and no means of cooking them. After the first day out an arrangement was made whereby Walter Butler, the cook for B company, was to have the use of the crew's galley to make coffee for the three Springfield companies. Walter did as well as he could under difficulties but ofttimes the water used in making the coffee was so poor in quality that the concoction was not exactly palatable. But it was better than ship's water.

The men messed as best they could. The officers had their meals in the dining saloon, paying $1 a day for them and they were not over luxurious. Neither were their quarters, for with the entire brigade on board the staterooms were insufficient to accommodate them all and they were forced to double up and in some instances three officers were assigned to one room and forced to "bunk" as best they could.

Many of the officers and men were just out of hospitals, and for them the voyage was a harder trial than those who were officially in good health. The ship's hospital was established on the aft deck and was protected from the elements only by canvas awnings and during the two or three times it rained during the voyage the sick men were drenched as they lay in their cots or hammocks. Surgeon Gates and Dr. Piersons, the contract surgeons who had done so much for our regiment in front of Santiago, were indefatigable in their attendance upon our sick and so were the hospital stewards, but the medical supplies were as usual insufficient and the accommodations entirely inadequate. Two men were detailed each day to assist in caring for the sick men from their companies and while of course they meant to do all they could for their comrades their performance very often fell far short of their intentions. Naturally the sick men were often peevish and troublesome and it cannot be said that the lot of the attendants was a very pleasant one.

On our second day out occurred the first death in the regiment, Sergeant Harold B. Wentworth of C company, who had been ill with typhoid fever and malaria. His body was buried at sea a few hours after death and the sad event was the first of a series during the voyage. Private George Higgins of F company was the next victim, his death occurring on the 15th.

August 17th was a black day for the Second. At 12.30 that morning Second Lieut. Harry J. Vesper of B company died after a long illness, with gastritis and malaria. He was a very sick man when brought on board but was nursed and cared for as tenderly as possible during the voyage. Private James Ryan of B was detailed as his attendant and was constantly with him, but even the best of care could not have saved him. The same day his body, wrapped in the folds of the American flag, was lowered into the deep, the Mobile being hove to for the purpose. The band of the 22d regiment played appropriate airs and Chaplain Wellwood of the Second conducted the services. The burial was nearly off Cape Hatteras. Lieut. Vesper, who was one of the most popular officers of the regiment, met his fate bravely and died in merciful ignorance of the fact that his brother, Private Paul Vesper of B company, had died a few days before the regiment left Cuba. At that time Lieut. Vesper was ill in the division hospital and it was deemed best to keep the knowledge of his brother's fate from him.

On this same day another B company man, Wagoner Paul J. Kingston, answered his final roll call, dying in the afternoon. Privates Earle C. Clark of H company and Franklin W. Manning of M company, made up the death roll for the day and their bodies were given to the sea.

On the 18th Privates Charles H. Cranston and Henry C. Collins, both of I company of Northampton, died and on the 20th just before we landed at Montauk Point Sergeant Ryder of E company passed away. On the voyage from Santiago to Montauk our regiment lost ten, one officer and nine men, and it is no wonder that the Mobile was referred to as a "death ship."

It is no wonder either, under these circumstances, that the men became depressed. Cooped up in an ill-smelling hold during the night, fed on unsuitable food and seeing the bodies of their comrades cast overboard day after day it was not strange that they became blue. But happily the voyage did not last long for on the afternoon of the 19th we sighted Montauk Point and knew that in a day or two we would be on good United States soil once more.

It was night when the Mobile cast anchor and early the next morning she was towed into what we supposed was quarantine. We passed several steamers with the yellow quarantine flag hoisted at their sterns and after a while the Mobile anchored and some quarantine officers came aboard and inspected the passengers and crew. Fortunately this ceremony did not last long and when it was over the Mobile was brought alongside a wharf as we in our innocence supposed to allow us to land.

But as it happened we were not to land that day. On the wharf were sentries and those of "Ours" who happened to get as far as the wharf were at once driven back. Neither was any one allowed at first to come aboard. As we swung in the stream before the Mobile got to the wharf a small boat containing some Springfield newspaper men attempted to get within reach of the Mobile, but she was ordered away and at the wharf it was some time before anybody was allowed to come aboard the Mobile. The first Springfield man we saw was Dr. David Clark, the surgeon for years of the Second while it was in the militia service. He finally came on board and was at once surrounded by the men of the three Springfield companies so that it was some little time before he made his way to the quarterdeck, where Col. Clark and the officers were awaiting him. He brought plenty of news for us and much information concerning Montauk Point and the arrangement of the camps there. At the same time came aboard baskets of sandwiches and fruit which Dr. Clark had provided. Thanks to the kindness of Dr. Clark many messages were sent from the ship to the anxious ones at home announcing the safe arrival of the Mobile and that the senders were well.

It was not until the next day that we were allowed to land and it was a sad spectacle to watch the disembarkation of the gallant Second from the ship. The men who were able to walk got down the steep gang plank in some kind of order and after an attempt at regimental formation, marched up to the quarantine camp, a distance of some two and a half miles, over the very roughest kind of a road. The sick were transported in mule wagons and they did not find the ride a very pleasant one. On arrival at the camp it was found all laid out with large wall tents arranged in company streets and the majority of the tents equipped with board floors, a luxury we had not experienced for many moons. Rough sinks had been made in rear of the company streets and supplies of soft bread, fruits and milk were waiting for us. A number of the sick officers and men were taken directly over to the hospitals and it began to look as if things might be half decent after all.

CHAPTER XVII

WE AND OUR FRIENDS ENJOY OURSELVES AT CAMP WIKOFF, MONTAUK POINT.

FROM the beginning it was evident that our lines in Camp Wikoff were to be cast in more pleasant places than had been the case since we left Lakeland in June. To be sure the detention camp was not an abode of princely luxury and there were shortcomings in plenty about it, but there was an honest effort to care for our comfort. There were but few of the officers and men in our regiment in good health and even the men who did not go to the hospitals were in bad shape physically, but the knowledge of the fact that we were on United States soil at last and that but a short time would elapse before we would be en route for home was better than medicine. Then, too, there was the great improvement in our food, which was worth something, and there was the presence of our friends from Springfield, including some who had made all manner of sacrifices and had endured toil, discomforts and trouble to get to us with help and cheer.

No one can doubt but what it was the full intent of those in authority at Washington to treat the returned soldiers from Cuba in the best possible manner, but it is a matter of common knowledge that as a paving material for a certain warm place good intentions is the very best material yet devised by the arch enemy of mankind. The performance at Montauk fell far short of the promise and this was aided by the over officiousness of some very young and very fresh officers who had no idea beyond the blind following of red tape regulations no matter what might happen. It was to these officers that the delay and vexatious troubles experienced by Dr. David Clark of Springfield in his mission of mercy to us of the Second can be attributed and others associated with him had to face the same difficulties. The story of how Dr. Clark, Lieut. T. A. Sweeney and others were "held up" at the mouth of the rapid fire guns of the converted yacht Aileen by one Lieut. Rhodes, whose name is still cursed by every Second regiment man, is still fresh in the minds of all of us and it was only when the presumptuous young officer was made to realize that he was not the only thing that ever happened that the supplies sent to us by loving hands in Springfield reached us. There is the memory too of the long and weary hours Dr. Clark spent underneath the pier at Montauk in order to remain inside the guard lines and be on hand to greet us when our ship came in. There are the memories of the good work done for us by our old surgeon when the Second was a militia regiment, Major Brown of North Adams, and of Lieut. Sweeney, E. S. Bradford, P. H. Quinn, Charles Lathrop as the representative of Dr. D. J. Brown, T. W. Hyde, and last but by no means least of Frank P. Frost of Springfield, who as the personal representative of Henry S. Lee, worked like a beaver day and night. The Springfield newspaper men, too, should not be forgotten and the thanks of many a poor fellow are due to H. L. Hines, G. H. Atwood and Frank Lee of the *Union* and to H. K. Regal of the *Republican* and T. W. Burgess of the *Homestead* for many kindnesses and unfailing sympathy.

The sad scenes attending the disembarkation of the Second from the Mobile will not be forgotten for many a day by those who witnessed or participated in them. A number of the sick men were taken off late in the afternoon of the 19th, but when dusk fell Gen. Young, the commander of the camp, refused to allow any more to be brought ashore until the next day. The next morning the exodus from the ship began at an early hour and continued until at last we were all ashore. First came the sick in a ghastly procession down the steep gang planks and into the ambulances which were to convey them to the hospitals and the sight of the poor fellows was pathetic in the extreme. The sick ashore, then came those able to walk or totter and these men, the majority of them wrecks of their once vigorous selves, dragged themselves to the pier laden down with their baggage and fell in for the march to the camp. Those unable to walk were piled into mule wagons and the procession started.

It was not a long march, but it was a fatiguing one for the men and they were glad when the big wall tents assigned to the Second appeared. This was the "detention" camp for in the eyes of the medical officers we were still suspects even if we had passed quarantine, and we were to be isolated for five days. It was not a bad camp. The tents were new and clean and many of them were provided with board floors, a luxury that reminded us of our militia days at South Framingham. It had been the intention of the war department to provide straw for us to sleep on but like many other intentions it was not fulfilled until Secretary Alger happened to visit the camp of the Second and found no straw. Then some came along in a hurry. There were cooking outfits, too, and the days of the canned roast beef and the other constituents of the palatable and nourishing (?) travel ration were numbered. In their place came the appetizing beef stew, the roast beef, soft bread and cool milk. There were also canned delicacies, and fruits, and tobacco in plenty. In fact, there were too many good things for some of the boys, as the hospital records attest.

It is needless to say that the hospitals were filled.

They were overcrowded, and that, too, in spite of the fact that additions were put on as fast as possible. The hospitals were of canvas but with raised floors and were equipped with cots. What the emotions of the sick boys were when they actually found themselves lying on a bed and between clean white sheets, and tended by kind and devoted nurses can be imagined. Not only that but they were given plenty of nourishing food and medicine was in plenty. After the lack of everything of the hospitals in Cuba the contrast was sharp, even though the Montauk hospitals lacked some things. As for the nurses and the doctors there was nothing they were unwilling to do to help the sick. Many of the nurses were Sisters of Charity or Sisters of Mercy, others were from the Red Cross society, others volunteers, but all were actuated by the same motives, and worked unremittingly to do all in their power for the boys. Some of the doctors were army surgeons and others were contract surgeons, but all worked alike. Then, too, there were any number of volunteer hospital assistants, all zealous to help us, some of them a little too much so, and it was a rare thing for the sick men in a hospital ward to lack for attention. Diet kitchens were established and a system of looking after convalescent and furloughed soldiers was established. In this work the noble efforts of the Massachusetts Volunteer Aid Association was pre-eminent and there are none of us who will forget what its representatives did, not only at Camp Wikoff but after our return to our homes. Not only did the society work among the soldiers from Massachusetts, but many a regular soldier was aided and comforted by its representatives.

Under the influence of proper care and food the men in the hospitals and the camps began to improve and though many died, yet more recovered. As soon as a soldier inmate of the hospital was anywhere near convalescence he was given a furlough to his home and transportation furnished him. At first these furloughs were only for ten days but after a bit they were lengthened to 30 days so that when the Second came to leave Montauk a good percentage of the officers and men had preceded it home. A large number of the sick men were taken from the camp hospital and sent to New York, New London, New Haven and other places where the local hospitals had opened their doors to the soldiers and where the care they received was in some respects better than that possible under the crowded conditions at Montauk.

In spite or all that could be done at Montauk there were many instances of individual hardship and although it seemed as if there were at least two or three people anxious and willing to look after every soldier yet there were cases of apparently unnecessary suffering. Soldiers discharged from the hospitals as convalescent would be sent to the depot at Montauk, a good two miles from the hospital, on foot and would be compelled to wait for hours in the hot sun before they could get transportation orders. At the depot there were often good men and women with cans of milk or lemonade and food, but even their zealous efforts could not prevent some suffering. All this was perhaps inseparable from the overcrowded condition of the camp and hospitals and the fact that there were not nearly enough officers to do the work properly.

On the 24th the regiment was released from quarantine and moved from the detention to the general camp. By this time rumors that we were to be furloughed and sent home were rife again and the date was finally fixed for the 26th. Meanwhile there had been some important visitors in our camp, including Col. Roosevelt, Secretary of War Alger and Gen. Wheeler and they all had good words to say for the Second. Also there were many visitors from Springfield and Western Massachusetts and the men were fed upon all kinds of delicacies, in some cases to the detriment of their health.

Musician Frank P. Jones of K company was the only Springfield man to die in Montauk, his death occuring on the

27th, after he had suffered for days with malarial fever of the Cuban type. He had not been ill in Cuba but the seeds of the disease lodged in his system there and in his weak condition when we landed at Montauk he was unable to resist it. We heard while at Montauk of the death in Cuba of Private Arthur M. Burnham of K and there were many regrets among his comrades. Private Burnham was ill when the regiment left Santiago for home and so was left behind.

On the 25th verbal orders furloughing the Second for 60 days were recieved and the regiment was ordered to be in readiness the next day to proceed home. At the expiration of the furlough the regiment was to be mustered out at South Framingham but this was afterwards changed to Springfield. The officers and men were all ready on the 26th to go home and the night before had been spent in packing up and putting everything in shape. The rifles and equipments had been turned in and the morning was eagerly anticipated. There was much disappointment when the day came and there were no signs of an immediate movement from the camp. Hour after hour passed and when it was finally ascertained that the departure was deferred to the next day because of a lack of transportation, there was nothing but disappointment from the commanding officer down to the privates. But the Second had by this time learned resignation and so the men waited through the long day and the equally long night for the word that the boat which was to convey the regiment to New London was ready.

The night of the 26th was made memorable by a wild stampede of a number of horses of the cavalry through the camp of the Second. The animals were being led to water and in some manner became frightened and getting away from the man in charge ran pell mell through the company streets of the regiment, upsetting stacks of arms and tents and leaving everything in much disorder. Fortunately no one was injured.

There was but little sleep in the camp that night. The boys were too much excited over the prospect of being at home on the morrow to care much for slumber, and they were up long before reveille sounded. Breakfast was hastily cooked and eaten and the outfit, or what was left of it, fell in for the march to the boat, some three miles away. There were ambulances for the sick and these were filled again and again. The men able to march were not numerous, and the companies did not have full ranks by any means. The men were without arms and clad in all sorts of uniforms, the yellow and blue Khaki predominating, although there were some who preferred the old militia blue uniforms they had worn from South Framingham. The regiment finally started for the pier amid the cheers of the 22d and other regiments it passed, and a short time after embarking was once more on the water but bound for home this time. The sick men who were unable to stand the journey were left in the hospital and those allowed to go were carefully looked after.

Arrived at New London the regiment fell at once into good hands. The people of that city had known of its coming and delegations were on hand when the boat came in, with food and refreshments for the boys. Meanwhile preparations had been made by the militia authorities of the state, and the people of Springfield and other places interested in the Second, to look after the men. Gen. Dalton had sent a detail of staff officers to Springfield with full power as to expenses to see that the returning soldiers who had shed credit upon Massachusetts were properly looked after, and a special train had been made up to go to New London to bring them on from there. Food and refreshments were taken on the train, and representatives of state and city were on board to render all possible assistance. The trip was a comparatively short one. At Palmer the three Worcester companies and F of Gardner were transferred to a train for their destination while the other companies came on to Springfield.

CHAPTER XVIII.

IN WHICH IS TOLD HOW WE PREPARE TO QUIT UNCLE SAM'S SERVICE.

THE home coming of Springfield's soldiers was not as glittering or gay a spectacle as had been counted upon by those who watched us march away on the morning of May 3d. That morning was a rainy and disagreeable one and there were many who consoled themselves in thinking of the rather tame character of our farewell, that when we returned the scene would be a far more cheerful and inspiriting one. It wasn't. For days and days, ever since the story of our losses at El Caney and San Juan had been known and the people had become somewhat familiar with the tales of sickness and suffering in Cuba and Camp Wikoff, the return of the boys had been anxiously awaited, but when the time came, when it was known for a certainty that the companies were to return, there was a common feeling that the occasion would be an ill timed one for any display of ceremony or pageantry, and as it became more known that the majority of the officers and men were in the poorest possible condition to stand the strain of an official, or even a semi-official welcome it was settled that their return was to be as quiet as possible.

The coming of the regiment from Montauk had been expected on the 26th and in anticipation a huge crowd had gathered at the union station to meet the soldiers. But the people were repaid for hours of waiting by the arrival only of a few men who had been furloughed from the hospitals. On the next day it was soon known that the regiment would surely arrive and long before the hour set for the special train to arrive from New London the station and its approaches were crowded with people, including the relatives and friends of the members, not only of the Springfield companies but of the companies from the other sections of Western Massachusetts. In view of the condition of the soldiers special efforts had been made to impress upon the people that the less excitement the men were made to undergo the better for them and to this end the station approaches were roped off and a large force of police was on hand to keep a passageway clear from the cars to the carriages which had been provided to bear the officers and men to their homes or wherever they felt inclined to go.

The state and the city co-operated well in making plans for the comfort of the returning soldiers. Gov. Wolcott was on hand when the special train rolled in and three members of his staff had been at work for several days previous assisting in the preparations for the reception of the men. Mayor Dickinson and the city officials had done everything in their power to aid the soldiers and with them at all times were the officers and members of the Volunteer Aid association and many private citizens, good men and women who labored zealously in the good cause. Others there were, too, not connected officially with state or city or with any society, but whose work was ably done and is never to be forgotten.

At 2.58 in the afternoon the train came in and the 10,000 people in waiting set up a cheer at the initiative of Gov. Wolcott. Then the people pressed hard against the ropes which marked the clear space on the platform through which the men were to go and the police officers had their hands full for a time in keeping them back. The north side waiting

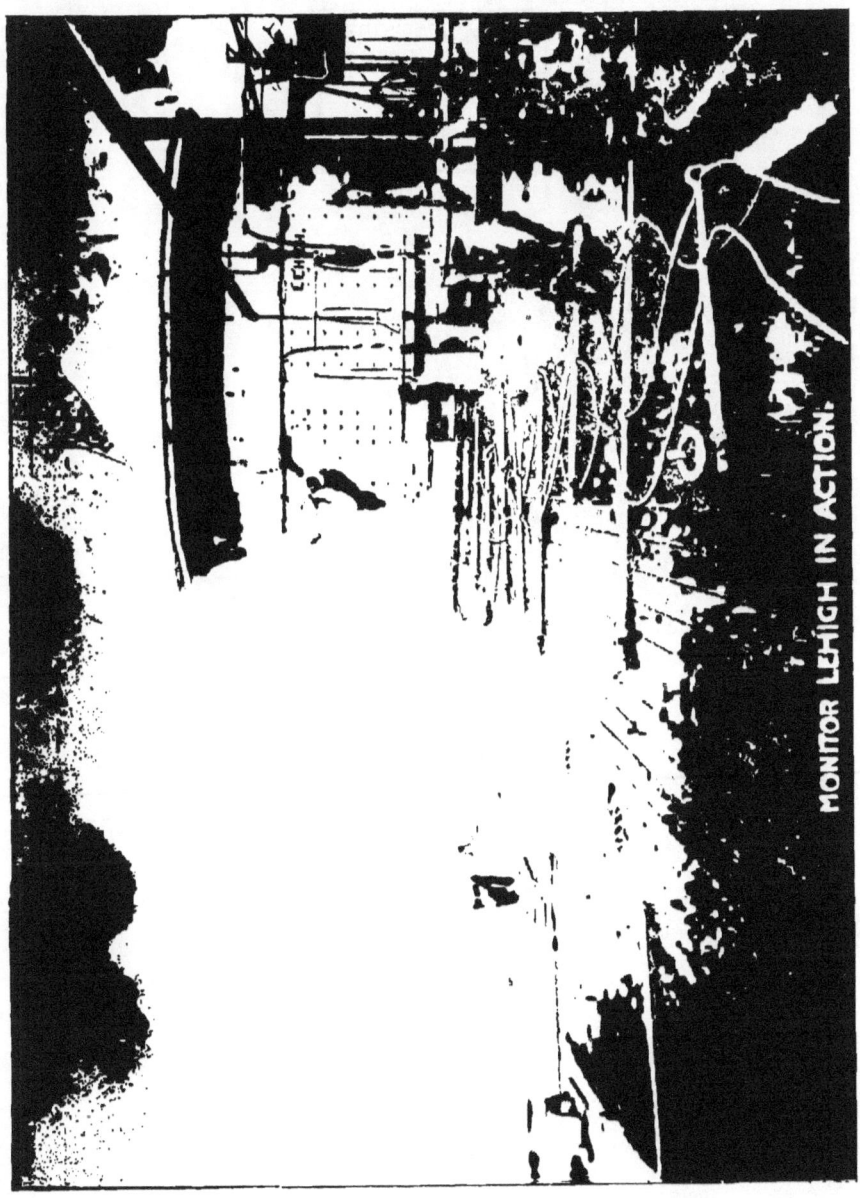

room had been cleared of occupants and outside were hundreds of public and private carriages waiting to carry the boys wherever they might wish. And in this one detail of carriages the thoughtfulness of the people of the city as well as their willingness to do all in their power for the boys of the Second were shown. Scores of them had volunteered eht use of their carriages that day and their offers had been gladly accepted, for in the majority of cases the men were hardly able to walk any distance, and a ride on a jolting electric car would not have been the best thing in the world for them. But there were carriages in plenty and the men were quickly and carefully conveyed either to their homes or the hospitals.

When the train stopped the people detailed to look after the disembarkation of the men at once got to work and the boys were quickly but tenderly taken through the waiting room and placed in the carriages. There were many who were unable to walk even this short distance unassisted, but in the majority of cases the men were so glad to be once more at home that the excitement kept them up and some lingered about on the platform, exchanging greetings with their relatives or friends in the crowd. A number of physicians were on hand to look after any of the men who were in immediate need of their attention and in many other ways provision had been made for all. The majority of the men were driven directly to their homes. Others went to the House of Mercy or the Springfield hospital.

The 10,000 or more people which greeted the returned ones did so in sober but cordial fashion. There was no demonstrative welcome, for common sense told the people that it would have been the worst thing possible for the men whom the crowd wanted to honor. They were in no condition to endure such a welcome and what they wanted was to get to their homes or a resting place as quickly as possible. When the Second went away it was in the blue uniform of the militia of Massachusetts. The men in the ranks were all young and vigorous and looked a composite picture of youth and strength. When they came back it was in the faded yellow khaki uniforms issued to them in Cuba, although a few still wore the blue. The natty uniforms of the officers were worn and soiled and the faces of all were haggard and in many cases the beards of veterans had replaced the smooth cheeks and chins of the militiaman. On almost every face was the badge of the campaign against the pestilential fevers of Cuba and the sunken cheek-bones and emaciated forms bore eloquent witness to the hardships and sufferings that had been undergone. It had been no holiday excursion for the gallant Second.

For days and weeks after the return the greatest interest was shown in the welfare of the men. Physicians placed their services at the disposal of the Volunteer Aid association and that body kept actively at work in its efforts to care for the men. Some of the boys were able to be out on the streets and in public places immediately after their arrival but in the majority of cases the men were glad enough to stay at home. Others were too ill to make their appearance in public, but those who were had no reason to complain of any lack of interest in them or their doings in Cuba. Columns were published daily in the newspapers concerning the condition of the sick men and the experiences of the well ones and the sight of the worn campaign uniform on the street was the occasion for a gathering of interested people. But as time went on the interest slackened, as it is in the nature of things so to be, the men showed a marked preference for citizens' dress instead of the uniform, and settled down again to the ordinary ways of life while waiting for their furloughs to expire and their muster out of the service of Uncle Sam.

There had been much concern expressed over the orders instructing the Second to assemble at South Framingham for muster-out and there was much satisfaction when it was known that the orders had been changed and that Springfield had been selected as the place. It was felt that this was fitting and proper and both the local members of the regiment and the people of the city were well pleased at the decision of the war department.

Meanwhile the men who had been left behind in Cuba, at Montauk and in hospitals at other places continued to arrive home and some time before the expiration of their furlough nearly all the surviving members of the Second were at home. From Cuba came the men who were left behind too sick to be moved when the regiment left for home and with them the men who had volunteered or been detailed to remain care for them. But all of them did not come. Privates Little and Stetson of G company had succumbed to disease and Dr. H. C. Bowen, the surgeon of the Second, was also a victim. He was in the division hospital when the regiment sailed and his death soon followed.

The fate which befell Dr. Bowen was a hard one. Enthusiastic to volunteer at the outbreak of the war he was assigned to duty as the surgeon of the Second with the rank of major and he had high hopes of a useful career in the army as had his friends for him. But he was totally without experience in army medical life, his assistant surgeons, though young and enthusiastic in their profession, were also inexperienced in this line of work and at the very outset he and they were thwarted and discouraged by their incessant conflicts with army red tape and the consequent difficulty in obtaining needed medical supplies for the regiment. Time and time again Major Bowen sent in requisition after requisition but no supplies came in answer to them and had it not been for the finely appointed medical and surgical outfit furnished by the state of Massachusetts the equipment of the Second would have been meager indeed. With these on hand the lack of proper government supplies was not seriously felt until after the landing in Cuba and then with the brilliancy which marked so many other features of the campaign, the Second's medical chest was not brought ashore, but was left on board the Knickerbocker until some time after the surrender of Santiago. As a result the medical supplies were short and though he tried again and again Major Bowen could obtain no more. Soon after he landed he was attacked by the malarial fever and though at first it was in a mild form it combined with the discouragements to which he had been subjected to make him low-spirited and not altogether a genial minister to the sick men or a companion at the mess. Directly after the battle of El Caney Assistant Surgeon Gates was taken from the Second and attached temporarily to the Fourth infantry, which regiment had no surgeon and Assistant Surgeon Hitchcock became ill so that the entire work of caring for the Second was thrown upon Major Bowen. This added to his other troubles and his own illness resulted in making the latter extremely serious and though he struggled against it for many weeks he was at last forced to give up. Before this he had manfully stuck to his post and tried in every way to do his duty but results of his failing health and his heavy burden of work were mistaken by many of the officers and men for lack of sympathetic feeling and for this he was criticized. This criticism was a mistaken one, for at bottom Major Bowen was of a kindly and sympathetic nature but it was his misfortune to have his illness and troubles put a veneer of mpatience upon his normal disposition and this conveyed the mistaken idea referred to above. In his service with the Second Major Bowen did all possible for a man to do and those who knew the heavy burden under which he toiled have always been willing to accord him the tribute he was justly entitled to. He died in the Second division hospital just outside of Santiago. Some months after his body was exhumed and sent to his family in Westfield. There was some mystery concerning the whereabouts of his watch and other effects but some time after his death they were accidentally discovered in New Orleans and restored to his parents.

At Montauk Point K company suffered a loss in the death of Musician Frank P. Jones, who succumbed to fever in the camp hospital August 27th. All through the campaign in Cuba Musician Jones not only kept himself well and his spirits up but his cheery speech did much to help his comrades. It was not until he reached Montauk that he gave in to the disease which laid so many of the Second low.

Even after the regiment had returned home and the sick men were being given the best of medical attention and care in their homes or in the hospitals the death angel did not cease. On Sept. 13th Corporal Patrick J. Noone of G company died at his home after a long illness with the fever and two days later his remains were escorted to the grave by his comrades and laid to rest after the three volleys which mark the soldier's burial had been fired. On October 8, Private Frank Burke of G died and was laid to rest in the same cemetery.

Meanwhile in both the Mercy and the Springfield hospitals all that was possible was being done for the sick "soldier boys," and physicians and nurses were untiring in their efforts. Both institutions had many soldier patients and they will long remember the devoted care and kindnesses they received.

All this time preparations for the muster-out of the Second had been going steadily on. It had been settled that the outfit was to be formally discharged from the United States service in Springfield and on Sept. 28th First Lieut. Oliver Edwards, 11th Infantry U. S. A., came on to assist in the work preliminary to muster-out. There was considerable to be done in the way of getting ready for the ceremony and there were many things to be explained to both officers and men before all was in readiness. In the effort to have everything clearly understood and all the "kinks" straightened out Lieut. Edwards was untiring and he made a most favorable impression upon all with whom his duties brought him in contact.

CHAPTER XIX.

WE BECOME PLAIN CITIZENS ONCE MORE AND SQUARE ACCOUNTS WITH UNCLE SAM.

OCTOBER 3d, 1898, is one of the "star" days in the history of the Second, that being the day on which we ceased to be soldiers of the United States and became plain and humble citizens once more. Incidentally it was something of a day for Springfield for one of the features of the muster-out was a brief parade of the regiment from the railway station to the state armory, where the exercises occurred. Before that, the armory had been for some time the scene of much activity. The furlough of the regiment, given it at Montauk, had expired October 24th, and for the rest of the time preceding muster-out the officers and men were required to make the armory their home during the day. Their meals were served there, a contract being made with a Springfield caterer, and it can be said that the daily menu was far more satisfactory than those we had in the campaign although the government paid for both. During this period, the officers and men were also required to appear in uniform and the streets took on a decidedly military appearance. Much interest was shown by the people of the city in everything that pertained to the muster-out and the armory had many visitors daily. But it was all play in those days for some of the officers and men. There is a lot of red tape and formality connected with putting volunteer organizations out of the United States service, and there was plenty of work to be done in making out rolls and all sorts of papers, so that those detailed for this work were kept busy for many days.

Finally on the 3d of October, all the companies of the Second were assembled in Springfield, the local companies marching to the railway station to meet them and after passing in review before the city officials at the city hall, the regiment marched to the armory for muster-out. The parade, the first appearance of the Second since it left for the front, brought out thousands of people to watch the men who had done good service on a foreign soil, and had watered it with the blood of many who had marched away on the morning of May 3d. The regiment presented a curious sight in some respects and as a spectacle it must be said the affair was not an altogether happy one. The men were without rifles or equipments, some wore the faded khaki uniform issued just before leaving Cuba, others the old blue outfits of the Massachusetts militia and the ranks were thinner than when the regiment left South Framingham. There seemed to be a chill in the air, too, and instead of applause there was subdued comment on the appearance of the men as they marched past.

Surely the men did not look like ballroom soldiers. The uniforms were in many cases ill-fitting and soiled, the marching was not done with the precision of some crack national guard organizations which did not go to the front, and the faces of the majority of the officers and men wore the yellow signal of service in a pestilential climate. But this in itself ought to have been warrant for some outburst of satisfaction in the gallant deeds of the regiment instead of curious stares and the silence of wonderment. However, there were sporadic cases of applause and as the men did not much care whether they received any or not, they found little fault with

The Prairie

the lack of it. Only the members of the companies from outside the city wondered mildly what it all meant, and if after all it would not have been as well to have stayed at home and not have tried to stand by the flag when men were wanted.

The ceremonies at the armory were informal enough. Each company was mustered out in turn by Lieut. Col. E. M. Weaver of the Fifth Massachusetts U. S. V.. who as a lieutenant in the Second U. S. Artillery had mustered us in at South Framingham on May 3d. He was assisted by Lieut. Edwards and it did not take very long to put each company "out of business" as United States Volunteers. The company was formed, the men answered to their names and took position in the same manner as when mustered in, and this over the company commander was informed that the company was mustered out and that discharge papers for each man would be provided.

But the discharge papers did not come that day nor for several days. The paymaster had failed to arrive with the funds and until these were distributed the men had but little use for discharge papers. It was explained that the reason for delay on the paymaster's part was due to errors in the rolls sent in from a few of the companies and as the men wanted their three months pay and allowances rather more than discharges, it is no wonder if some unkind things were said as to the paymaster and these companies.

It was not until November 17th that the long looked for pay arrived, and the companies were ordered to once more assemble at the armory, this time for the purpose of settling accounts with Uncle Sam. This operation was simple enough, yet very interesting to the recipients of the contents of the small and dingy valise of the paymaster. The three months' pay with the allowances for clothing and ration money made quite a sizable sum for the great majority of the men, and the nice new greenbacks which they received were not refused. With the money came the discharge papers as a sure enough sign that we were no longer soldiers of the United States. Many of the officers and men failed, however, to settle up with Major Sherman on the 17th. Some of the officers had not squared their accounts with the war department and in some cases they were obliged to wait a considerable time before they accounted for every bit of property they were held responsible for and complied with all the red tape. A number of the men were not able to be on hand, owing to sickness and other causes, when Major Sherman finally arrived and they were likewise forced to wait. An interesting episode of "paying off" time was the breezy disagreement between Major Sherman and Capt. McDonald of B company, over the former's refusal to pay some eight men of the latter's company, who had, it seems, signed one pay roll and supposed that everything was all right. As it happened, when Major Sherman came to Springfield, he failed to bring the correct roll for B company, and insisted that the members should sign a new one. This was done, but as the eight men referred to were out of the city, they were unable to sign, and when they appeared for their pay, were told they would have to wait for some time. The majority of the men needed the money and needed it badly, but although Capt. McDonald exhausted every effort to obtain it for them, it was not till quite a while had elapsed that they were paid. The opportunity afforded Capt. McDonald for some caustic criticisms of the workings of the war department was not allowed to pass.

In those days it was a great thing to be a returned soldier as was instanced in the cases of several of the boys who were members of more or less secret organizations. It got to be a common thing for these associations to show their appreciation of their soldier members by presenting them with money or badges, or some token of esteem, and a number of the men who served with the Springfield companies are wearing medals or badges thus presented. Probably none of them was prouder of his medal than Private Morris Grenowitz of B company who had the distinction of being the only Hebrew in the three Springfield companies. He was a member of the Young Men's Hebrew Association, and soon after his return the association held a public reception in his honor and presented him with a check for a small sum of money and a gold medal. Private Peter F. Boyer of B company was given a gold watch by the members of an organization to which he belonged and several of the other boys were similarly remembered, among them Private William Ferrier of G company who was given a handsome gold ring. A number of the members of the Springfield companies resided in West Springfield and the inhabitants of the village of Mittineague in that town honored their soldiers one evening by a big reception and entertainment with plenty of red fire, etc., included.

A largely attended public reception and flag presentation was held in the city hall, on the evening of November 3d, to which the officers and members of the Springfield companies, and their relatives and friends were invited and the hall was packed to the doors. Gov. Wolcott and members of his staff were present and the governor spoke, as did a number of the prominent citizens, all eulogizing the work of the regiment and paying a tribute to the officers and men who had failed to return. The tattered colors of the regiment were in evidence and their appearance in the hall was the signal for an outburst of applause. On this occasion the stands of colors purchased for each company in connection with the Fourth of July celebration of 1898, which never came off, were formally presented, and as the representatives of each of the companies advanced to receive the new and handsome flags, the audience broke into applause and cheers. These flags were bought with the proceeds of the sales of the Fourth of July badges which were to have been a feature of the celebration and a good sum was realized.

Previous to muster-out First Sergeant T. F. Burke of B company had been appointed on the recommendation of Col.

Clark as Second Lieutenant to fill the vacancy caused by the death of Lieut. Harry J. Vesper.

Immediately following the muster-out Dr. E. A. Gates, who had been promoted from Assistant Surgeon to Surgeon with the rank of Major, vice Bowen, deceased, was ordered to Boston and Worcester to assist in the work of examining the men of other regiments to be mustered out. Assistant Surgeon Hitchcock was also ordered on this same duty. Dr. Hitchcock was attacked with a serious spinal trouble and for some months his life was despaired of. He finally recovered but not until after weary months of suffering.

Soon after the muster-out of the Second the provisional militia companies organized in the city during the war ceased practically to exist, although they were not formally disbanded for some time afterwards. The reorganization of the Second as a part of the Massachusetts Volunteer Militia did not start until after its muster out of the United States service and it was at one time freely predicted that the work of reorganization would be the hardest task ever experienced by those in charge. It looked so at times, but in spite of the croakers and pessimists who asserted that it was likely that the Second would never be the same regiment again the reorganization was quietly and successfully effected and it was not long before the outfit was once again in its old form. A surprisingly large number of the officers and men who had served in the war remained in the regiment and this was especially the case in the three Springfield companies, G and B having more of the veterans than K. The state granted the regiment a 30 days' furlough dating from Nov. 3 to Dec. 3 in order to allow time to get matters straightened out before its entrance upon a career of militia service again.

Meanwhile steps had been taken toward an expedition to go to Cuba and bring back the bodies of the dead of the Second. The co-operation of the cities and towns from which the regiment was recruited was obtained and a number of meetings were held in this city, representatives from Worcester, Holyoke, Northampton, Greenfield, Orange and Adams being present with authority from their respective cities and towns. After a number of meetings an expedition was organized which left for Cuba in January, 1899. The Springfield representatives were Lieut. T. F. Burke of B company, Lieut. Fred Jenks of K company, Private Dozilva Lamoreau of G company and Private Alfred Rose of B, the latter going as interpreter. The progress of the expedition was slow at first, owing to many difficulties connected with obtaining permission to disinter the bodies and of getting transportation, but thanks to incessant work and powerful influence these were at last disposed of and the party sailed from New York on Jan. 29. It was necessary to go first to Porto Rico and remain there some days but after Santiago was reached there was comparatively little trouble. The bodies of the Springfield men were all located and identified with one exception, that of Private Robert E. Kelly of G, who was fatally shot on the night of July 2d at San Juan. The bodies were encased in metallic coffins and on arrival in Springfield were given proper burial. An elaborate service was held over the body of Sergeant Richard H. Bearse of B company in the State Street Baptist church, representatives of the city government and the organizations of which he was a member as well as his own company, being present. The church was crowded with friends and the ceremonies were impressive. Before this the body of Musician Frank P. Jones of K had been brought on from Montauk and buried in Oak Grove cemetery after largely attended services in the State Street Methodist church. The bodies of the G company men were buried with military honors also and those of Privates Little and Stetson, whose relatives could not be found, were interred in a lot which the company purchased in the Springfield cemetery.

Twice within the year 1899 were the Springfield companies called together to go over again in memory the deeds of the previous year. For some time there had been desultory talk of public honors being paid to the dead of the companies and finally a memorial service was arranged for and was held in the city hall on Sunday afternoon, April 16. It was one of the most disagreeable days imaginable, a fall of mingled rain and snow filling the streets with slush, but despite this the building was jammed to suffocation. The platform was decorated with appropriate bunting and in front were representations of memorial tablets bearing the names of the officers and men of the companies who had given their lives in the cause. The war-worn regimental colors were brought on from Boston for the occasion and were draped in the rear of the platform. Affecting tributes were paid to the dead heroes and eulogies were pronounced by some of Springfield's most prominent citizens.

The camp of the First Brigade M. V. M. at South Framingham in August, 1899, brought the regiment once more onto the ground where it was mustered into the United States service the year before, but under much different circumstances than then. The ranks of the Second contained a very large percentage, a majority, in fact, of those who had gone out with it to Cuba and the red sleeve stripes indicating service in war were conspicuous on the blouses of the greater number of the men. At this time old friendships formed during the campaign were renewed and new ones formed.

On the occasion of the annual fall drill of the state militia in Boston in October Admiral George Dewey was the guest of the city and the event was also made the occasion of the formal "turning over" of the "war colors" to the state. The Second came in for no little share of the honors of the occasion, as well it might.

As time wore on after the return of the regiment from the fever stricken camps in Cuba the malarial poison left the bodies of the men and within six months afterwards the majority of them had regained their normal health. There were many, however, with whom the exposures and hardships of the campaign had raised havoc and to this day some show the effects of the short but eventful period when they were serving under the flag. The latest man in the Springfield companies to succumb to the ravages of disease contracted in the campaign was Private John L. Morehouse of K company, who died Nov. 12 of typhoid fever.

In October, 1899, a number of the officers and men of the Springfield companies who had served in the Cuban war began the organization of a camp of the Legion of Spanish War Veterans, an order patterned after the model of the Grand Army of the Republic and which it is to be hoped will be to the veterans of the war with Spain what the Grand Army is to the men who fought in the Civil war. The camp was named after Henry S. Lee of Springfield, whose splendid and self-sacrificing work for the benefit of the soldiers and sailors in the Spanish war will never be forgotten by them or the people.

Thus closes the record of Springfield's three infantry companies in the war with Spain. It is not a long chronicle but it is one in which the people of the City of Homes can always take a just pride. It is not confined to these companies alone either, for aside from the efficient duty performed by her company in the naval brigade, there were many individual enlistments in regular regiments and there was the splendid work done at the United States armory in turning out the arms with which the troops were equipped. As in the Civil war the works were run day and night and the force of employes trebled. There was good work done too at the recruiting station and it is not too much to say that Springfield was a prominent factor in the war from its beginning to its close. When the rebellion against the authority of the United States in the Phillippines broke out and volunteers were again called for Springfield again showed its patriotism. A number enlisted from this city in the famous 26th and among them were many of the men who had seen service in Cuba. Others went into the 46th and more would have gone had it been necessary. As always the city and its men young and old showed their loyalty to the flag, whether it led the way to the hills around Santiago or to the rice swamps and jungles of Luzon.

CHAPTER XX.

WHEREIN IS NARRATED THE ADVENTURES ON THE HIGH SEAS OF SPRINGFIELD'S SAILORS.

WHILE the land soldiers which Springfield furnished the government were enjoying themselves in Florida and Cuba and toying with the canned roast beef and other incidentals of a campaign, the Springfield marine contingent was not having an altogether lovely time. On the monitor Lehigh and the auxiliary cruiser Prairie there was work and hard work too in plenty but on the whole the rations and the quarters were better than those enjoyed by the infantry contingent. But the boys of H company, naval brigade, pined for active service and those on the Lehigh were aggrieved at not getting it while their comrades on the Prairie were roaming the seas on a fast ship in chase of of the enemy or doing blockade duty off the coasts of Cuba and Porto Rico. It was hard work for the Lehigh men to be cooped up on their old, "flat boat" in Boston harbor during the stirring times of the summer of 1898 but it is to their credit that although they grumbled at their lot as all good sailors do, yet they did their full duty and did it well.

The bringing of the Lehigh from the League Island navy yard to Boston Harbor was in itself something of an achievement for the tug which towed her broke down and the monitor was forced to proceed under her own steam, much to the surprise of those on the tug Clara Clorita. This happened at Vineyard Haven and from that point to Boston the Lehigh was cast off from the tug and was sailed the remainder of the way under her own steam and by her own crew. When the Lehigh left Philadelphia the navy yard officials were apprehensive of her behavior at sea as she was primarily a coast defence vessel but the naval brigade men in the monitor found no great trouble in sailing her.

The Lehigh reached Boston on May 5 and on the 9th the Springfield officers and men of the crew were given leaves of absence and furloughs to enable them to attend the presentation of "The Ensign" by Springfield amateurs at the Court Square theater for the benefit of the company fund. The crew included Lieut. J. K. Dexter, Lieut. (j. g.) W. O. Cohn, Ensign Walter S. Barr and Seamen W. A. Sabin, A. N. Luce, R. P. King, Paul H. Lathrop, L. E. Ladd, W. S. Johnson, W. F. Bright and R. H. B. Warburton. The presentation was a successful one in every way and netted quite a sum.

Meanwhile the Lehigh had been permanently detailed for duty in Boston harbor as a coast defence vessel and a disagreeable surprise was in store for some of the Springfield men when they returned from their furloughs. They were all anxious to re-enlist for service and had been assured by Capt. Weeks, commanding the naval brigade, that if they telegraphed to him their willingness to re-enlist before a certain hour on the 10th, places would be kept for them. But on their arrival on the ship on May 12th they found that there was only one vacancy left. Just how the mistake was made was never thoroughly explained, but it was suspected by the Springfield men that there was a scheme to shut as many of them as possible out in favor of some Boston naval militiamen. They felt it keenly and Lieut. Dexter succeeded in straightening out matters so that Coxswain Johnson and Seamen Bright and Warburton were re-enlisted. Sabin,

Luce and King had already done so and this left only Lathrop and Ladd out in the cold. In spite of their efforts they could not get in.

The officers suffered also from the fact that there were not places enough for all of them in the Lehigh's complement as a coast defense ship. Lieut. Cohn was offered the alternative of going on the waiting list or being reduced in rank to ensign. He chose the latter and remained with the ship but there was no place for Ensign Barr and he was placed on the waiting list and returned home to await orders. Later Lieut. Dexter was taken from the Lehigh and placed on the converted ferry boat "Governor Russell," the property of the City of Boston which had turned over to the government, as executive officer.

All this time the "Prairie dogs," as the crew of that vessel were dubbed by their less fortunate comrades, were having a fairly good time at the Brooklyn navy yard. Much time was spent there in fitting up the vessel as an auxiliary cruiser and until the work was well advanced the crew was lodged and fed in hotels and later in the navy yard barracks.

As it happened, Ralph H. Newcomb was the first of the Springfield men to reach the Prairie and report for duty. He was in Washington on a visit when orders were issued for H company to report at Brooklyn and when he was notified by Lieut. Crossman he lost no time in getting to that city and the navy yard, beating out his comrades by several hours.

Hammocks were "swung" on the Prairie for the first time on Saturday, May 7th, and from that time until muster-out in September hotel fare was a dream of the past to which the boys looked back with considerable regret. The Prairie, completely transformed into a war ship, left the navy yard and steamed down the harbor to Tomkinsville. This was on Friday, the 13th of May, but if there was any "hoodoo" it failed to work. The next day the Prairie steamed out to sea and had target practice, badly frightening some of the residents of the coast with the big guns. Late in the afternoon the Prairie gave chase to a suspicious craft which turned out to be an English tramp steamer.

The Prairie had been assigned to patrol duty on the North Atlantic coast with the San Francisco. The "Frisco" was sighted on the day following and both ships steamed into Provincetown and remained there for the next day, sailing out late in the afternoon. It is recorded that the sailors washed clothes during their stay in Provincetown and it is evident they were getting a taste of the life of a jolly tar. The regular patrol tour of the Prairie was from Provincetown north to some 40 miles above Boston, then south to Nantucket to Provincetown, meeting the San Francisco off the cape and obtaining mail.

These were not idle days by any means. What with battalion drills, inspection, target practice, painting ship and the regular routine of ship's work the long hours of duty passed quickly and the men were pretty well tired out as a rule when the time came to get into their hammocks. But the men of H company learned fast and soon accustomed themselves to life on one of Uncle Sam's war ships. The one thing they did not take to very kindly in the line of work was coaling ship and this came rather oftener than they had any relish for.

In the way of food there was little to complain of, although the fare was not Delmonico-like by any means. One of the mess cooks kept a diary of what he served up for every meal during the service of the Prairie and it shows that the menus, while probably simple enough to the men on board, would have been regarded as the acme of luxurious living by their brethren of the Second. A few samples are given: breakfast, June 10, Indian meal and coffee; dinner, soup, roast beef and potatoes; supper, hash and French toast. June 12th, breakfast, bacon and potatoes; dinner, sausages and potatoes; supper, beans, cold meat and sausages. The daily average was fully up to the samples given above.

Capt. Train of the Prairie was a disciplinarian and there were punishments meted out for various small offences. One man was deprived of shore liberty for three months for throwing swill out of a port hole. For smoking outside of "smoking hours" the customary punishment was 48 hours of extra duty, while for being late with hammocks the sentence was for the delinquents to parade the deck for an hour or two hours with the hammocks on their shoulders.

The Prairie sailed from Provincetown June 10th for a brief cruise southward, but returned on the 14th. The weather was very foggy during the cruise and on the 14th the ship came near running down an English tramp steamer passing within a boat's length of her.

On the 16th the Prairie sailed again from Provincetown for Delaware breakwater, arriving there on the 18th. The next day she sailed for New York, anchoring off Tompkinsville the 20th. Coaling ship was one of the innocent amusements of the day and the men stowed away 83 tons in the afternoon. Early next morning the sport was resumed and before breakfast 23 tons more had been put away in the bunkers, the record for the day being 182 tons. The next day the coal situation again took the attention of the crew but they finished the job. Shore liberty resulted in some of the men overstaying it and being shut off from any more during the stay. On Sunday, June 26th, the men got into blue dress for inspection but before the ceremony was over orders came to sail at once for Key West. Off came the blue suits and the men got into their "coal" suits again and finished coaling ship at 1.30 in the morning. The Prairie sailed for Key West on the 27th, arriving there June 1st. Her stay was short, for the same day she left with mail for the blockading squadron off Cuba and sighting the Amphitrite the next day transferred her mail to her. Later that day the Prairie gave the mail to the Newport, Montgomery, Vicksburg and Marietta. That afternoon the men on the Prairie saw the Marietta pick up a refugee from the shore and saw the guns from Morro Castle fire at her but fail to strike.

On July Fourth the men paraded in blue and fired the national salute. The Prairie for a day or two acted as flagship of the squadron during the absence of the Amphitrite at Key West.

On Tuesday, July 5th, the Hawk came alongside the Prairie with orders for the latter to proceed to Mariel, 23½ miles from Havana, and assist in the capture of a liner supposed to have been trying to run the blockade. The liner proved to be the Spanish transport Alphonso XII, with a large number of soldiers on board. She had tried to run the blockade but had been discovered and chased so sharply by a couple of the converted yachts attached to the blockading squadron that she was run ashore and lay head on. The troops and her crew had managed to get ashore by the time the Prairie came up, but it was not certain that she was not manned and several shots were sent at her from the starboard six-inch guns. After the fourth or fifth shot there was an explosion, evidently her magazine, and as she did not return the fire the Prairie ceased firing. During the firing a saucy little Spanish gunboat stuck her nose out of the harbor but a couple of six-inch shells settled her fate and she was sunk in quick time. The firing at the Alphonso XII was first-rate target practice and at long range, too, all the shells hitting her, although the range was 6600 yards.

On July 7th the Tecumseh brought a lot of mail from Key West for the Prairie and a good share of the day was put in in reading it. On the 9th a small shark was caught and some of the boys secured teeth as souvenirs.

Monday, July 11th, the Prairie was relieved of blockade duty off Mariel and ordered to Gibara with the Topeka, Mayflower and Badger, the Prairie being made the flagship of the squadron. The trip to Gibara was without special incidents and the ships arrived there on the 13th. Just as the blockaders appeared a schooner and two fishing smacks which were just coming out made haste to get back into the port. Blockade duty was kept up for several days and occasionally the ship would go in so close to the town that the people could be seen in the streets. The search-lights were used about every night and this work was pleasing to the men detailed for it.

The San Francisco arrived on the 17th and took off a lot of mail for the United States. Since leaving Havana the crew of the Prairie had not received any mail and were eagerly expecting some. On the 18th the supply of sugar gave out and this was keenly felt until some was procured. On the 20th the Maple, which had joined the squadron, caught a small sloop with a crew of four men and laden with tobacco, making the first prize of the tour.

One of the marine detail on the Prairie was a Springfield man named John Fenton and on the 21st he was the victim of a severe accident caused by the slipping of a six-inch shell from his hands at gun practice. The shell landed on his foot, badly crushing it.

This same day a delegation of the prominent citizens of Gibara came out in a small boat and offered to surrender the town as the Spanish garrison was about to leave and the inhabitants were afraid of the negroes in the vicinity. On receiving the offer the Prairie steamed to Nipe bay where the Topeka was found engaged in shelling the town. The Dupont took a message to the Topeka and the Prairie returned to Gibara. From a Cuban who came out in a dory it was learned that the inhabitants had raised an American flag over the town and were anxious that a force be landed to take possession of the place. It was also learned that the town was short of provisions. The Cuban's heart was gladdened by the gift of hardtack, canned meat, corn and coffee. On the

25th the Mangrove brought orders to proceed to Guantanamo bay and coal up at once. At Guantanamo fresh meat and also newspapers a week or two old were received.

Wednesday, July 27th, marked the close of the third month of service of the Prairie's crew and as if to celebrate the event the Supply came in with a lot of provisions. The work of coaling ship was begun on the night of the 25th and did not cease until the 27th, the men standing their regular watches and doing their trick with the coal as if it was nothing unusual.

The Prairie sailed from Guantanamo bay on the evening of the 27th and reached San Juan, Porto Rico, on the 29th. Some ammunition brought from Guantanamo for the cruiser New Orleans was transferred to her in boats. The Prairie did not stay long at San Juan but sailed for Ponce on the other side of the island on the 31st, arriving there the next day. Troops were being landed at Ponce and the roadstead was filled with war ships and transports. One of the transports became stuck on a bar outside the light-house and the Prairie had hard work getting her off the bar. A lot of mangoes brought aboard resulted in a number of the men being made ill from indulging too freely in the fruit. The soldiers on the transport Massachusetts, the one which was stuck, were taken on board the Prairie and fed, being landed the next day.

News of the cessation of hostilities reached the ship August 5th and was received at first with incredulity. The night of Friday, August 12th, was made memorable by Burgess tumbling out of his hammock three times in rapid succession. "Rags," the canine mascot, had become subject to fits and was assisted to commit suicide one day while in the harbor.

The Prairie received orders to sail for the United States and on August 18th left for Santiago, arriving there the 20th. The ship left Santiago the 21st, with three companies of the Seventh infantry on board. All went well until the 25th,

when a heavy fog came on and the Prairie ran aground near
Amagansett Point, 15 miles from Montauk Point. There
was considerable confusion, of course, but the Prairie was
handled well. All the boats were lowered and two kedge
anchors were put out, one from the starboard quarter and
the other from the starboard forecastle. The boats were out
all night and it was not until at high tide the next day that
the Prairie was hauled off by the tug Brittania and a light-
house tender. The soldiers were landed and taken to Montauk Point. After being hauled off the Prairie sailed for
Montauk Point, arriving there early in the evening. At
Montauk the Prairie was put into quarantine until the 28th.
Hardly was she out of quarantine before she steamed to
Newport and from there to Fall River, where a warm reception was given the Fall River men on board the ship. That
evening the Fall River and New Bedford men went ashore
but the Springfield contingent was kept on board, much to
their disappointment. On the 30th the Prairie left Fall River
and steamed down to Newport, the event of the evening
being the playing of the "Fu-Fu" band. The next day the
ship started for New York and remained there until the 19th,
when she went to Delaware Breakwater. Rumors of discharge began to agitate the crew soon after arriving in New
York and Capt. Train went to Washington to confer with
the Navy Department concerning it but returned with no
definite knowledge of the exact time the muster-out would
take place. From Delaware Breakwater the Prairie steamed
up to the League Island navy yard where some of the guns
were taken off and transferred to the New York. During
the stay in New York and at League Island the "Rough
Riders" made several successful initiations.

Sunday, September 25, hammocks were lashed for the last
time and after the dunnage had been loaded on a tug, the
crew mustered and gave three cheers for Capt. Train and
Lieuts. Stone and Stimpson. This done, the crew bade good

bye to the Prairie and went ashore, going to Jersey City by train. After a brief trip on a ferry, the Fall River boat was boarded for the trip to that city and Boston. The latter place was reached about 10 o'clock Monday morning and after passing in review before the governor at the state house the Prairie men proceeded to the receiving ship Wabash, where they were furloughed until the following Wednesday. The boys enjoyed themselves hugely in Boston until Wednesday, when they were mustered out and given their discharges from the service of the United States.

At 9.15 that evening, the Springfield part of the crew arrived home and were given an enthusiastic welcome in which red fire and fireworks played a prominent part. At the armory the men were greeted by glad relatives and soon dispersed to their homes plain naval militiamen once more after doing their full duty to Uncle Sam and serving him well.

Lieut. H. S Crossman, who went out with the Prairie detail remained on the ship until she was ordered south, when he and some of the other officers were sent out on special duty. He was assigned to duty as recruiting officer on the Minnesota and remained there until a short time before the dismissal of the Prairie's crew from the service.

Lieut. J. K. Dexter was detailed from duty on the Lehigh to duty as navigator on the converted ferry boat, Gov. Russell, and ordered to take her to Key West. The trip was an eventful one, for the Gov. Russell as a war boat was a fearfully and wonderfully constructed piece of marine architecture, and there were times when it was a question whether she would ever reach a port or not. But finally she was navigated as far as Newport News, and after looking her carefully over, the naval authorities decided that it was not wise to expose her again to the high seas.

After muster-out of the Lehigh detail H company was once more at home and it was not long before the reorganization of the command as a part of the state militia was begun and successfully carried out, a good number of the officers and men who had seen service remaining. Today the company is once more in its old position of the best all-round company in the Massachusetts naval brigade.

On October 27th, a number of prominent citizens tendered H company a banquet at Hotel Worthy, and the occasion will long be remembered as a very pleasant one. During the evening the handsome silk American flag, purchased for the company by citizens, was presented by Rev. Dr. P. S. Moxom.

ROSTER.

FIELD STAFF AND NON-COMMISSIONED STAFF.

COLONEL, EMBURY P. CLARK.
MAJOR, FREDERICK G. SOUTHMAYD.
ADJUTANT, FIRST LIEUT. PAUL R. HAWKINS.
QUARTERMASTER, FIRST LIEUT. EDWARD E. SAWTELL.
MAJOR AND SURGEON, HENRY C. BOWEN.
MAJOR AND SURGEON, ERNEST A. GATES.

SERGEANT-MAJOR, ROBERT N. INGERSOL.
QUARTERMASTER-SERGEANT, ROSS L. LUSK.
HOSPITAL STEWARD, EDSON P. HOWES.

G. COMPANY.

CAPTAIN, JOHN J. LEONARD.
FIRST LIEUTENANT, WILLIAM C. HAYES,
SECOND LIEUTENANT, EDWARD J. LEYDEN,
FIRST SERGEANT, WILLIAM BUTEMENT.
SERGEANTS, JEREMIAH F. SCULLY.
        JOSEPH N. LOVELY.
        WALTER W. WARD.
        JOSEPH A. MURPHY.
        JAMES A. GIBBONS.
CORPORALS, ROBERT A. ROSS.
        PATRICK J. NOONE.
        MICHAEL J. MCHALE.
        FRANK C. KEATING, Chicopee Falls.
        NATALINE GARDELLA.
        ERNEST E. ROBINSON.

Musicians, Patrick J. O'Connell,
  Robert D. Cargill.
Wagoner, James R. Shene.
Artificer, Benjamin A. Seamans.

PRIVATES

Frank A. Anderson
Timothy T. Austin
Elmer B. Barrowcliffe
Frank J. Barsalow
Daniel J. Bellamy
Wilbur G. Brassard, Thompsonville
James H. Bresnahan
Patrick J. Bresnan
Alfred C. Brownell
Francis C. Burke
Thomas Burke
Henry T. Conrad
George W. Campbell
Thomas M. Conlin
William E. Coolidge
Timothy J. Crowley
William R. Dillon, W. Sp'f'd
John H. Dunn
George E. Easton
William Ferrier
Charles R. Fisher
Theodore Gelinas, Holyoke
Frank M. Hannon
Patrick J. Hayes
Andrew F. Higgins
Frank N. Hunt
Robert G. Kelly
Edward K. Lathrop
Henry H. Lawler
Dozilva P. Lamoreaux, Chicopee
Andrew Little
Christopher T. Lovett
John J. Mahoney, W. Sp'f'd
Thomas F. Mahoney
George H. Markham
John B. Mandeville
Ernest P. Marble
Dennis F. McCarthy
Henry E. Merchant
Louis Monteverde
Fred H. Morrill
Carl A. Mueller
James J. O'Brien
Charles A. Nelson
John J. O'Leary
Arthur H. Packard
Walter A. Packard
Jacob Peterson
George A. Richmond
William J. Rooney
William J. Root
Jeremiah J. Shea
Cyrus A. Shufelt
Henry J. Slattery
Fred S. Stetson
John E. Tobin
Henry B. Whitmore
Samuel Wilson

B COMPANY.

CAPTAIN, HENRY MCDONALD.
FIRST LIEUTENANT, WILLIAM J. YOUNG.
SECOND LIEUTENANT, HARRY J. VESPER.
SECOND LIEUTENANT, THOMAS F. BURKE.
SERGEANTS, RICHARD H. BEARSE.
  SAMUEL E. SMITH.
  GEORGE J. MCKEOWN.
  JOHN J. O'CONNELL.
  EVERETT W. WILCOX.
CORPORALS, FRANK A. WAKEFIELD.
  MELVIN H. RANSOM.
  RICHARD B. BLANEY.
  MICHAEL J. DONAHUE.
  JOHN B. FULTON.
  THOMAS F. HANDY.
MUSICIANS, HENRY F. LADBURY.
  BERNARD E. COMEY.
WAGONER, PAUL J. KINGSTON.
ARTIFICER, ORVIN E. ALBERTS.

PRIVATES

Charles H. Ashley
John Bryson
Peter F. Boyer
William F. Barton
William J. Barton
John M. Carey
William F. Childs
Matthew J. Clark
Theophile J. Champagne
Clarence E. Chapman
William W. Chadbourne
Albert M. Chandler
Donald A. McPhee
William J. Mack
Daniel J. Moriarty
Frank C. Mattoon
Axel Mahlstrom, East Longmeadow
John J. Malone
Howard S. Meyrick, Agawam
John J. O'Donnell
Arthur M. Partridge
Giles S. Potter, Pittsfield

Lewis R. Dikeman
Frank F. Dingman
Robert D. Draper
Daniel S. Devine
Albert R. Dunn
George DeGray
John K. DeLoach
Frank L. Edson
Henry T. Ellis
James F. Ferrier
Ellsworth Frey
Eugene B. Grenier
Morris Grenowitz
Joseph Genereaux
John C. Hurley
Robert J. F. Judd
Michael F. Kelleher
Ernest J. Monseau

Alwin B. Richter
Christopher J. Riordan
Thos. R. Rooney, Westfield
Wilmore S. Riopel
Matthew M. P. Ryan
James C. Ryan
Henry P. Roberts
Frank X. Rivers
Clarence B. Ross
Harry H. Richards, West
    Springfield
Alfred E. Rose
John J. Smith
Frank Twohey, Worcester
Paul L. Vesper
Harry C. Wakefield
Ernest C. Whitcomb
Edwin W. Wright

K COMPANY.

CAPTAIN, WILLIAM S. WARRINER.

FIRST LIEUTENANT, PHILIP C. POWERS.

SECOND LIEUTENANT, HARRY H. PARKHURST

FIRST SERGEANT, ARTHUR J. BERRY.

SERGEANTS, FRED A. JENKS, Chicopee.
    G. BURTON HALL.
    DAVID A. TURNER.
    J. LEWIS KELLY.
    HYATT W. AVERY.

CORPORALS, WILLIAM C. PIPER.
    THOMAS C. BOONE.
    BURDETT A. MADISON.

WILLIAM E. TURNER.
ALBERT MARSDEN.
BERT F. NICHOLS.
MUSICIANS, FRNAK P. JONES.
LOUIS P. CASTALDINI.
WAGONER, FRANK N. BOULE.
ARTIFICER, WILSON C. EMERY.

PRIVATES.

Ernest L. Alderman
Edward N. Aiken
Horace W. Allen
Wallace H. Brown
George L. Bates
Ralph A. Barkman
Arthur N. Broulette
Arthur M. Burnham
Albert J. Brunell
Michael E. Breck
James W. Britton
James A. Brazzil
Frank L. Carr
Arthur L. Chapman
William C. Colvin
Alwin A. Cameron
George S. Creeley
William R. Dunse
Edwin A. Elwell
Horatio M. Field
Wm. J. Fish, W. Springfield
Harry D. Fisher
Ralph Fisk
Herman H. Fuller
Julian B. Hawkes
Louis H. Hall
Frank B. Hendricks
George Hallier
Edward R. Hubbard

Charles Hoadley
Irving J. Johnson
Ward Lathrop
Michael R. Lyons
Everett W. Luther
Myron W. Maynard
Charles E. McLeod
Wm. C. McCulloch, Chicopee
Frank E. Moody
John L. Morehouse
Homer G. Munson
Samuel W. Nesbitt
Charles Owens
A. L. Potter
George W. Potter
Walter J. Reardon
Phillip H. Robinson
William E. Stephens
George E. Sollace
Edgar W. Snell
Harry J. Symonds
Alfred Stone
Robert B. Terrell
Nicholas D. Vassilli
William J. Walsh
Harry O. Wilkins
Joseph G. Woodbury
Henry Wright, Jr.
William A. Webb

HENRY S. LEE

H COMPANY NAVAL BRIGADE.

Name	Rating	Ship
Lieut. Jenness K. Dexter		U. S. S. Gov. Russell
Lieut. (j. g.) Henry S. Crossman		U. S. S. Prairie
Lieut. (j. g.) William O. Cohn		U. S. S. Lehigh
William A. Dearden, Boatswain's Mate, 2d class		Prairie
William Owens, Gunner's Mate, 2d class		"
James A. Turnbull, Gunner's Mate, 3d class		"
Curtis H. Jennings, Gunner's Mate, 3d class		"
Arthur H. Strong, Chief Q. M.		Saturn
Winfred A. Sabin, Coxswain		Lehigh
Herbert E. Burns, Bayman		Prairie
Ernest F. Gilbert, Shipwright		"
George H. Nobbs, Pay Yeoman		"
Albert M. Pease, Cook		"

SEAMEN.

William H. Brundett	Prairie	George W. Lyman	Prairie
Weston F. Bright	"	Irving C. Lombra	"
A. W. Blauvelt	"	George L. Meacham	"
Webster C. Clark	"	Charles B. Miller	"
Lewis B. Clark	"	Ralph Newcomb	"
Winfred W. Crosier	"	Guy A. Preble	"
Charles Crosier	"	Gilbert G. Patnode	"
Charles W. Dearden	"	Goulding S. Patnode	"
Lawrence W. Erricson	"	Walter Swazey	"
Arthur J. C. Fischer	"	Edwin S. Smith	"
Robert C. Goodale	"	Fred C. Steele	"
Robert P. King	Lehigh	McClellan E. Streeter	"
Albert N. Luce	Prairie	Rupert H. B. Warburton	
Howard Loomis	"		Lehigh
Ward H. Long	"	Robert H. Wheeler	Prairie
Frank Ladd	"	Henry W. Watson	"

THE ROLL OF HONOR.

Henry C. Bowen, Major and Surgeon, died in Second Division Hospital, Santiago, August 13, of malarial fever.

G COMPANY

Corporal Patrick J. Noone, died in Springfield, September 20, 1898, typhoid fever.

Private George A. Richmond, died in field hospital near El Caney, July 1, 1898, of wound in head.

Private Walter A. Packard, killed on field, El Caney, July 1, 1898.

Private Robert G. Kelly, died in division hospital of wound received in action July 2d, at San Juan.

Private Francis A. Burke, died at Springfield, October 24, 1898.

Private Andrew Little, died in second division hospital, Santiago, August 22, 1898.

Private Fred S. Stetson, died in second division hospital, Santiago, August 24, 1898.

B COMPANY.

Second Lieutenant Harry J. Vesper, died on S. S. Mobile, August 17, 1898, of gastric enteritis.

Quartermaster Sergeant Richard H. Bearse, died in camp before Santiago, August 1, 1898, of malarial fever.

Wagoner Paul J. Kingston, died on S. S. Mobile, August 27, 1898, of malarial fever.

Private John J. Malone, died in field hospital, July 5, 1898, of wound received at El Caney, July 1.

Private Paul Vesper, died in camp before Santiago, August 10, 1898, of malarial fever.

K COMPANY.

Corporal William C. Piper, died in second division hospital, August 5, 1898.

Corporal Thomas C. Boone, died in Springfield, March 19, 1899.

Musician Frank P. Jones, died at Montauk Point, L. I., August 27, 1898.

Private Frank E. Moody, killed on field, July 1, 1898, at El Caney.

Private Arthur M. Burnham, died in division hospital, Santiago, August 18, 1898, of typhoid fever.

Private Michael R. Lyons, died in Springfield, April 20, 1899.

Private George S. Creley, died in Springfield, June 28, 1899.

Private John L. Morehouse, died in Springfield, Nevember 12, 1899.

Since the muster-out three more of Springfield's contingent, all K company men, have answered the final roll call. Corporal Thomas C. Boone died in Massachusetts general hospital at Boston, March 19, 1899, and Private Michael R. Lyons at Springfield, April 20, Private George C. Creley died June 25, at his home after a long illness. Private John L. Morehouse died in Springfield, November 12, 1889.

SPRINGFIELD'S DEAD HEROES.

HENRY C. BOWEN.

Henry C. Bowen, major and surgeon of the Second regiment, died in the Second Division hospital, near Santiago, after making a gallant fight against sickness and death, not only for himself but for the regiment under his care. It is not too much to say that but for the heavy burden he was under with the care of over 800 sick and dying men on his hands, he might have recovered from the Cuban fever and been alive to-day, but as it was he succumbed. It was his misfortune to go to the front ignorant of the red tape which forms an even more effectual barrier to individual action than did the Spanish barbed wire to our troops, and it was this same red tape which was indirectly responsible for his death. When the regiment was in its worst condition in front of Santiago, when he was alone in the work of caring for the sick and dying, he found it next to impossible to obtain needed medical supplies for his men, and yet knew he was held responsible for their welfare. It is not to be wondered at under these circumstances that he grew nervous and irritable, and repelled rather than attracted those who tried to help him. The wonder of it was, that sick in body and mind as he was, he bore up as long as he did. But he did what he could and gave his health, and strength, and life in his duty.

Major Bowen was born in Castle Creek, N. Y., the son of Dr. Charles W. Bowen of Westfield, and he studied in the public schools there and at Wilbraham academy. He gained his medical education in the University of New York and served in Bellevue hospital for eighteen months and in the Broome street lying-in hospital. He began practice in

Springfield in 1894 and was fast reaching a high place in his profession when the war broke out. At the time of his appointment he was a member of the surgical staff of the Mercy hospital where he was liked by patients and officials.

HARRY J. VESPER.

Second Lieutenant Harry J. Vesper of B company, came of fighting stock, his father, O. R. Vesper, of Springfield, being a one armed veteran of the civil war. Harry was born in Springfield and was 31 years of age when he died on the Mobile. He studied in the public schools, leaving the high school to enter the employ of the Springfield Homestead. There he rose by steady industry and ability, to be head of the mailing department and business manager of the electrotyping department. For several years he had been deeply interested in the militia and had enlisted in B company, rising through the grades of corporal and sergeant to the second lieutenantcy, to which he was elected and commissioned May 11, 1896. For two years he had served as adjutant of the first battalion of the regiment, and was popular with everyone in the command.

RICHARD H. BEARSE.

The news of the death of no member of the Second was received in Springfield with more regret than that of Sergeant "Dickie" Bearse of B company. A member of the company for several years, he was known and liked by all the officers and men of the Springfield companies, for to know "Dick" Bearse was to like him With his pride in B company and the regiment, not to speak of his patriotism, it was only natural he should be anxious to go to the front with the Second, and he did so, although he had to twice overcome the examining surgeon's objections. In camp and on the march he was cheerful and helpful and at El Caney he was up with the best of them. But all the while the hardships and toils of the campaign were sapping his vitality, and when the deadly calentura came, he had no strength left to resist it, but simply laid down and died. In him B company and the Second lost one of their best. Sergeant Bearse was the son of Mr. and Mrs. Leon Bearse and was 24 years of age. His body was brought home and interred in the family lot in Oak Grove cemetery, after such a funeral as has seldom been witnessed in Springfield, an outpouring of grief from hundreds of friends.

WILLIAM C. PIPER.

Corporal William C. Piper of K, was born at Marysville, O., in 1874, and his father is a well known lawyer and probate judge of that state. Corporal Piper came to Springfield in 1895 as manager of the Stetson Shoe store and had charge of the establishment at the time he was mustered in to the United States service. He enlisted in K company in 1897.

FRANK P. JONES.

Musician Frank P. Jones of K, and one of the best fellows in the Second, died in the hospital at Camp Wikoff, August 27, after passing through all the hardships of the campaign in Cuba without being seriously ill. He was a native of Ludlow, Mass., and was 21 years of age. He had served in K for three years and though opposed by his parents, could not be kept from enlisting as a volunteer when the call came for troops. Of a cheerful, happy disposition, he did much in the dark days of sickness and death in the camp before Santiago, to help his comrades, and his example helped many a sick man.

PAUL J. KINGSTON.

Wagoner Paul J. Kingston, B company, was an efficient soldier and well liked member of the command. He was 24 years of age when he died on the Mobile and was the son of George Kingston, an expressman. He was serving the third year of his enlistment in B when the war came and at once volunteered to go to the front.

PAUL VESPER.

Private Paul Vesper of B was younger than his brother, Lieut. Harry J. Vesper, but had many of the qualities which made the latter so well liked. He was serving his first enlistment in B company when the war came, and promptly expressed a desire to volunteer. He died in the camp before Santiago, August 10, 1898.

ROBERT G. KELLY.

Robert G. Kelly was the third G company man to fall in the fighting in front of Santiago. At 10 o'clock on the night of July 2d, the crashing of rifle volleys and the screams of shells awoke the Second from the sleep of fatigue, and the officers and men rushed to the crest of the hill behind which they had bivouacked. The attack was to the right of the Second's position, but while waiting for orders the regiment had to stand the rain of scattering shot and Kelly was the first to be hit. The bullet struck him in the left cheek, going through and lodging in the muscles of the other side. He was taken to the division hospital and died there July 15. He was the son of Samuel Kelly of Springfield and enlisted just before the Second was ordered to South Framingham.

ARTHUR M. BURNHAM.

Private Arthur M. Burnham of K was the son of George M. Burnham, a well known contractor and builder of Springfield. Arthur was born in 1876 and studied in the public schools. He was popular with his school fellows and with all who knew him. For three years previous to the breaking out of the war he had been associated with his father in business. He enlisted in K company soon after its transfer to Springfield and after serving three years, left the company, a short time before the war broke out. He was one of the first of the former members to reenlist when it was known that war was certain and bore himself manfully through the campaign. He was ill with typhoid when the regiment left Cuba and was obliged to be left behind.

FRED A. STETSON.

Fred A. Stetson enlisted in G company at the outbreak of the war and served faithfully until he was attacked by the disease which laid him low, only a day or two after his comrades had left Cuba for home. He was employed in Springfield when he enlisted, but had only been in the city a short time, and had no near relatives living so far as known. He was 24 years old.

JOHN J. MALONE.

John J. Malone, fatally wounded at El Caney, was a member of B company and had been for two years previous to the outbreak of the war. He was a bright, cheerful young fellow and was well liked by his acquaintances as well as by his comrades. His parents died during his childhood and John made his home with a relative. He was employed in the Homestead office. At El Caney, Malone was one of the first men hit, the fatal bullet striking him within a few moments after B company had taken its position with the 22d. He died in the field hospital.

FRANK E. MOODY.

Frank E. Moody of K company, killed in action at El Caney, was the son of Mr. and Mrs. C. H. Moody of Springfield and was 20 years old when he enlisted in K, only a few days before the regiment left for South Framingham. He was shot soon after B and K companies took position on the right flank of the 22d.

ARTHUR HOWARD PACKARD.

Killed instantly at El Caney, July 1, 1898. He was the son of Mrs. Helen N. Packard, who, the wife of a soldier of the civil war, saw her two sons go to the front in the war with Spain, both being members of G company. Arthur would have been 19 years of age in November, 1898, and had been employed in the Homestead office. When only 17 he enlisted in G company and was well liked by his comrades. When the war came Arthur insisted on being one of the men to go with the company. Through the campaign he was soldierly and cheerful and his bright, if sometimes caustic sayings, did much to help his comrades. He was on the advanced firing line of the Second in the squad under Lieut. Leyden when the fatal bullet struck him and he died instantly

GEORGE A. RICHMOND.

George A. Richmond was one of the oldest members of G company and was born in Springfield. He enlisted in 1887, and remained a member of the company for several years. When it was seen that war was coming, Richmond was one of the first to apply to Capt. Leonard for a place in the ranks and joined the company at South Framingham. At El Caney Richmond was with Lieut. Leyden's squad, and was shot through the head early in the engagement. Willing hands bore him to the improvised field hospital where he lay in agony for several hours before death came. He was comforted and consoled by Chaplain Fitzgerald of the 22d, who took his last messages. Richmond's mother died in his early youth and he had made his home with relatives. He had been employed in the Springfield post office. He took a small camera with him to Cuba and made a number of pictures.

FRANCIS A. BURKE.

Private Francis A. Burke of G company, who died at the House of Mercy hospital, October 8, 1898, was the son of Thomas Burke and resided at 196 Spring street. He was employed as a clerk in the store of Forbes & Wallace and was well liked by his associates. He was 22 years of age. As a youth he took much interest in military matters and was for some time a member of the Cathedral cadets. Later he enlisted in G company and had served some time when the war broke out. He promptly volunteered and served well in the campaign.

THOMAS C. BOONE.

The circumstances surrounding the death of Sergeant Thomas C. Boone, who went to the front with K company, but was transferred to the U. S. Signal Corps, were particularly sad as at the time his many friends supposed he was practically recovered from the terrible experience he underwent while in the service. Boone died in the Mass. General Hospital, Boston, on March 19, 1899, after a comparatively brief illness. He was a native of Maryland, being born in Annapolis in 1876, and came to Springfield in 1894, enlisting in K company soon after his coming here. At South Framingham Boone was appointed a corporal by Capt. Warriner, but the number of these positions in the companies being reduced Boone was obliged to serve as a private. Soon after the arrival of the Second at Tampa he was transferred to the signal corps with the rank of sergeant. He was an expert telegrapher and was selected for that reason. On July 2d he with Col. Drew and Major Maxfield were in the war balloon at San Juan and while the balloon was at a height of 2700 feet and was being taken over a creek it was pierced by three pieces of shrapnel from the Spanish lines and fell. The basket caught in the top of a tree and Boone was caught in the anchor and hung suspended over the stream for a long time with the iron hook pressing into his side. Then he fell into the water. He was badly injured, but did not realize it at the time. A few days later he was sent to the hospital, but while being conveyed there in a mule team the vehicle was upset and he was again injured. On his return to the United States through an error on the part of some officer he was accused of desertion but after several months the stain was taken away and he received an honorable discharge. Boone was a popular member of the company and also popular among a large number of friends.

MICHAEL R. LYONS.

Michael R. Lyons of K company, died in the Mercy hospital, Springfield, April 20th, 1899, just a year from the time he enlisted and after making a gallant fight against the effects of the hardships he underwent in Cuba. He was a well-liked member of the company and made an excellent soldier, doing his duty quietly and faithfully. All through the campaign, although ill at times, he was cheerful and uncomplaining and his example was not lost on his comrades. His body was taken to Palmer for burial. His parents and brothers reside in Springfield.

ANDREW LITTLE.

Andrew Little was one of the "recruits" of G company, he having gone to the camp at South Framingham with the first batch of extra men assembled in Springfield after it was known that several vacancies had been caused in the company through rejections by the surgeons. He lived in Middlebury, Vermont, but had been employed in Springfield for some time. During the campaign he served as assistant company cook and stood the hardships and exposure fairly well until a short time before the regiment left Santiago for the United States

GEORGE C. CRELEY.

George C. Creley, 21, was one of the last men of K company to die, his death being due to consumption contracted in service in Cuba. His death occurred June 28, 1899, after a long illness. Creley left a father and a sister, the former living in Springfield. He was a recruit, enlisting in K as soon as there was an opportunity and his service was faithful.

JOHN L. MOREHOUSE.

The last member of K company to pass away up to the time of issuing this volume, was Private John L. Morehouse who died Nov. 12, 1899, after an illness of several weeks. He was a cousin of Lieut. H. H. Parkhurst of K and was well liked by his comrades, being easily one of the most popular members of the company. He was 29 years of age and aside from cousins, had no near relatives.

www.ingramcontent.com/pod-product-compliance
Lightning Source LLC
Chambersburg PA
CBHW020817230426
43666CB00007B/1041